Healthy Relationships

OVERCOME ANXIETY, COUPLE
CONFLICTS, INSECURITY
AND DEPRESSION WITHOUT
THERAPY. STOP JEALOUSY
AND NEGATIVE THINKING.
LEARN HOW TO HAVE A HAPPY
RELATIONSHIP WITH ANYONE.

RACHAEL CHAPMAN

TABLE OF CONTENTS

When men and women are able to respect and accept their differences then love has a chance to blossom.

DR. JOHN GRAY

INTRODUCTION

Relationships are like kites – you can let them soar high in the sky and see how they do or you can control them by keeping a tight grip on them. They are also like flowers that bloom in full swing when nurtured with love and care. As humans, we all crave love, affection, and attention. We crave human touch, we crave meaningful conversations, we crave those little moments of joy and pride where we see our partners doing things to make us happy.

However, relationships lose their spark over time. Couples lose their energy and passion they had when they were dating. It may begin to feel like your partner is no longer the same person. One day we are happy, and the other day we are not. One day we are on Cloud Nine, and the next day we are filled with doubt and unhappiness. There is no in-between to how we feel, and this happens when communication suffocates.

The healthy and consistent conversation is the cornerstone of every relationship. It is the glue that holds the relationship together. A lack of it can ruin even the most perfect of couples. Therefore, in order to lead a blissful and jovial life, it is important that communication is improved.

Lucky for you, in this book, we tackle some of the biggest and most common challenges couples face. We talk about the importance of listening, what it comprises of and how we can become better listeners to our partners. We also learn how to handle arguments and conflicts in a less heated and calm manner and talk about some of the biggest issues couples mostly fight about.

Later on, we present our take on how we can share our opinions without feeling judged or criticized. We also understand the need for open communications and the exchange of ideas and how it helps partners come closer to each other.

As we move forward, we deal with the core of the book, which is improving communication, and advise you on some of the best and most fun couple-therapy exercises to enjoy together. We also discuss issues like building a deeper bond with everyday routines that your partner appreciates, the need for appreciation and ways to show it, etc.

All in all, if you feel like you are at a dead-end in your relationship or feel trapped in a loveless marriage, pick up this book before you turn to therapy. This has answers to some of the most mind-boggling questions you have regarding your spouse that no therapist will discuss in this much detail. Don't believe us? Take a look at it yourself.

CHAPTER - 1
LISTENING EFFECTIVELY –
LEND ME YOUR EAR

Not one of us accepts that they aren't a good listener. Everyone thinks they are, but what if the other person disagrees? When couples come for therapies, their primary concern is the lack of communication between the two parties, which can arise due to several reasons. But do you know that one of those reasons can be a lack of active listening? Listening is a skill that each one of us must cultivate and nourish. It becomes even more important when one steps into a relationship. As important as physical intimacy is in any relationship, so is emotional intimacy. That breeds with communication and how good or bad it is between the couples.

If you have been feeling like you and your partner are growing distant because you two rarely share anything anymore or you think that your partner can be a better listener, then in this chapter, we shall be addressing this concern and looking at the reasons as well as the ways to curtail this gap between the two of you. Hopefully, both of you will identify where the problem lies and move forward to work on it.

UNDERSTANDING ACTIVE LISTENING AND ITS SIGNIFICANCE

Do you happen to throw a fit or construct a counter-argument every time you two try to communicate with each other? If so, then it means both of you need to find some other means of communicating that is less alarming than this.

This is where active listening comes in. Active listening is usually one of the first homework couples get after their first session with a counselor. Well, there wouldn't have been a need for one if you had just done it on your own, right?

Active listening is a form of listening that involves an empathic ear to the other person. Often known as reflective listening, it consulates giving full attention to the other person's grief, ideas, opinions, just concerns, and fears. It is more than just hearing someone's story. It is more about being there physically, emotionally, and verbally.

Ideally, research stresses that we need a shift in stimulation every 20 minutes, but thanks to our smartphone screens and the push notifications, our attention span has declined to less than 20 seconds. Meaning, we are unable to hold or listen to any conversation past the 20-second milestone, which is both shocking and sad.

10 As human beings, we are bound to be preoccupied

with our own trail of thoughts. Even when we are in a conversation with someone, we are easily distracted because of some external or internal influence and lose attention towards what the other person is saying. This is such commonality with couples who have spent some good years together. Does it ever feel that your partner zones out halfway through the conversation? It must definitely bother you and become a reason enough to initiate a fight. Not only that, it can damage the trust you two hold for one another. What happens next is that you begin to seek that validation and empathy from someone other than your partner and that is when the actual problem starts. You both become immune to each other. You find someone else vocalizes your feelings and your partner gets away with avoiding the conversation. This is where a lack of communication occurs.

So how do you work it out and hope that it doesn't come to this?

Engage in active listening. Be there for one another. There is always so much stress hanging around, just piling up in your chest. The stress from work, stress from the kids, the stress about the finances, etc. Talk and discuss. More importantly, if your partner comes seeking someone to talk to, make sure you are there. They should know you are there for them. Show them that they have your support and love. Tell them that you feel bad there is nothing they can do about it (in case the stress is about something you can't help with).

"But my partner never shares anything with me, what

do I do now?"

Initiate. There is nothing wrong with a little probing. Ask them how their day was. Did they have fun? Would they like to go out for dessert? (If they seem stressed.) In a relationship, there is no I. It won't make you a smaller person if you seek their attention sometimes. Of course, trying to gain their attention all the time is an entirely different problem, but whenever you feel like, in doing so, you will be bending to them, don't. You are in this together and thus make every possible effort to stay together. There are days when we both have to lift each other, open up to each other, and make room for some meaningful conversation to stem.

You know what will happen when you do that?

It will eliminate the blame from your relationship. A lot of times, it is only an ear that the partner needs, not advice, suggestions, or opinions. They just want someone to vent out so that they can lift the burden from their shoulders. When you become an active listener without any strings attached, you help them reach a solution that comes from their own mind. Sometimes, we all just need a thumbs up, a token of appreciation for our thoughts, and active listening offers exactly that.

Active listening makes conversations smoother and allows them to fall in a safe, understandable and comfortable space.

Active listening has less to do with what you should say and more with being able to sit through someone's plight and offer humility. This is an ideal tool when dealing with partners who are shy or emotionally unavailable to open up frankly with their significant other.

It also eliminates judgment. Most of the times we don't speak our mind fearful of being judged. Even if this is the start of your relationship and you have just started dating the guy/girl, you might tone down on the heavy and personal details about yourself. It's natural for you to feel that way because you are still in the phase where you want your partner to like you. However, what you don't realize is that the more open you are, the better the chances of your partner doing the same and speaking their mind without the fear of being judged.

Moreover, it cultivates intimacy. As humans, we all like attention, the feeling of being seen, listened to, and understood. It becomes pivotal in relationships and can nurture intimacy. Intimacy is a connection that opens up more opportunities to come closer – both physically and mentally.

When combined with empathy, active listening can help create a deeper and more nourishing bond between couples as well as dating partners. Since it requires engagement and interest, it makes the person feel valued and, thus, appreciated. This empathy further accelerates active listening and helps partners build better interpersonal relationships.

WHAT IS ACTIVE LISTENING COMPRISED OF?

A lot of people don't understand the basics of active listening and what it is comprised of. To keep it simple and short, this is what active listening looks like.

- It is nonjudgmental and neutral.

- It requires patience and moments of complete silence.

- It involves verbal as well as non-verbal feedback, such as eye contact, smiling, mirroring, etc.

- It includes questions when it is appropriate.

- It can involve asking for clarification.

- It includes the reflection of what is being said.

- It summarizes.

While at it, it is also important to know what active listening isn't like.

- Not showing respect and empathy.

- Being distracted in your own thoughts and not listening attentively.

- Hearing superficial meaning only.

- Avoiding eye contact.

- Interrupting.

- Ignoring.

- Trying to top their story with one of your own.

- Forgetting what the person said before.

- Rushing them.

- Asking unimportant questions.

- Pretending to pay attention.

- Not asking for clarification when needed.

WILL YOU EVER TELL ME WHAT'S IN YOUR HEAD?

When you aren't listening or paying attention to the verbal and non-verbal cues from your partner, communication is bound to suffer. A lack of communication is a progression towards divorce for many. We all are different in the ways we express our thoughts and concerns. This is because we come from different families raised differently. Some partners who come from loud families tend to express their emotions similarly. At the same time, partners who come from conservative and strict families often resort to keeping things to themselves. This is a caveat as no fruitful conversation happens. When we keep our emotions piled up, it can rile up frustration and we start to crack. When it all comes out all at once, it can become reason enough for a fight.

Since your partner is supposedly the closest person to you, sharing your concerns is a primary need. Not doing so will affect your work, life at home, and even your sex life. Want us to further convince you why you should never shut yourself out emotionally and verbally from your partner? Take a look!

Emotional compatibility takes a toll. When we limit the amount of communication, we close all doors for emotional compatibility, which is a requisite for both physical and mental health. Talking is the easiest way to connect with someone and, surprisingly, also the hardest for many. Lack of communication can fade away from your lover over time – something you don't want to happen.

When couples don't speak to each other, it can sometimes **lead to misjudgments and misunderstandings.** It becomes easier to just make an assumption about your partner's reaction to what you have on your mind. When you don't communicate your plans or thoughts outspokenly, you leave them with doubts about self-assume. For instance, imagine the husband doesn't know that the wife has plans with her girlfriends after work and will get home late. Will it be wrong on the husband's part to think that she is doing something she isn't supposed to be doing? Our minds are wired to think the worse first. When she comes home, you can expect a fight. Now, had she communicated about her plans in the morning, this wouldn't have happened and all the tensions, doubts, and negative thinking could have been avoided.

Think of it in another way. You are in the mood for sex, but your partner flatly refuses and goes to sleep without giving you an explanation. You would spend all night thinking why he/she doesn't want to have sex, are they seeing someone else, are they bored, do they not find you attractive anymore, and so on and so on. The simplest explanation could have just been fatigue or a rough day at work, but since it wasn't communicated, the couple may experience a rift.

Your sex life will also suffer because of it. Sexual problems, such as lack of orgasm for a woman, can be a reason for frustration. This leads to a lack of interest in the whole act of intimacy. However, how do you expect your partner to get the clue if you don't communicate it to him? During the start of a relationship, many partners feel hesitant to make the first move. Lack of initiation without any communication can make your partner think that you don't want it as much as they do. Couples who are open about their expectations regarding sex can enjoy it more and reach their respective orgasms. Play out your sexual fantasies and talk about what turns you on verbally, so that your partner can incorporate more of it the next time you get busy.

Lack of communication can also be mistaken for a **lack of compromise.** Every relationship, be it personal or professional, is built on some levels of compromise. An employee may work late shifts to complete a project and get two days off after its completion by the employer. That's them compromising equally. A compromise shouldn't put one partner under stress. It should benefit you both equally. Lack of conversation can lead to one thinking that the other one isn't ready to meet them halfway and, therefore, create feelings of resentment, anger, and disappointment. However, if both the parties place their cases and try to reach a middle ground, it can benefit both of them.

Lastly, when there is a lack of communication from either of the parties, partners seek validation elsewhere. They still have so much they need to talk about. So they turn to other ears and discuss their private matters with their family or friends. But not always does the best advice come from a stranger. What you and your partner have should remain between the two of you at all costs, unless it escalates to a point where an expert has to step in and resolve the issue. Couples who avoid communication amongst themselves are no less than two roommates living together.

CLASHES BETWEEN INTERESTS AND NO MUTUAL GROUND

We often see couples in movies and real-life who are similar down to the dot. Even their interests, hobbies, even their choices in politics, sports, movies, books, and food are the same. And then, some couples share no grounds of mutual interests whatsoever, like the couple in Pretty Woman or the couple in A Walk to Remember. They rarely have anything in common to talk about and yet they are the ones many people look up to. You know the couples who are complete opposites of each other, like one would be the high school prom queen and the guy would be a nerd or the guy is a popular hunk and the girl being the most unnoticeable woman in her class... You get the point, right?

When partners seek counseling in their marriage, a common complaint is that both of them have nothing in common to talk about. So it begs the question, is having common interests that important to sustain communication and active listening in a relationship? If yes, shouldn't all those couples who are like the different poles at the end of a magnet never find joy in their marriage? Shouldn't they already be arguing, or worse living like two strangers in the same room?

They should, shouldn't they? But, do they? They don't.

So if it isn't black or white, what is it? Is having mutual interests critical or can the couples do fine without them too? Let's take a look at whether it is important, and if it is, how are we going to address it for couples who suffer because of it.

Better yet, let's create a pros and cons list for the sake of the argument and see which one wins the bet.

Common Interests Matter

1. Shared interests breed passion. When you and your partner are both whole-heartedly into something, you are going to enjoy it more. It can create room for not only meaningful but passionate conversations because of common ground.

2. It helps initiate conversations. Common interests can be a great conversation starter and help partners get to know each other better. Also, it can make time together more interesting and worthy. For instance, if both the partners love art and craft, chances are they will be going on several trips to museums, historical sites, art galleries, etc. and be able to appreciate and critique it together. Imagine if one partner just has to be tagged along in all these. Would the conversations

be interesting? In fact, they would seem burdened and both the partners would experience guilt for feeling that way.

3. Some also believe that they are highly critical as the physical attraction only lasts so long. Eventually, the two of you will have to speak to each other, and lacking any common interests or hobbies will leave you with nothing to talk about.

No, They Don't

Those who think that common interests don't matter as much state the following reasons.

1. It gives each of you time to enjoy your own hobbies without being forced to do something you don't enjoy doing. Even those couples who seemed to be joined at the hip can have different interests, but they seem to get along with their differences just fine. The best part is that you don't have to give up any part of your personality because the other person doesn't feel like being a part of it. For instance, if you like to go to a yoga class and your boyfriend or partner doesn't, you don't have to give up going to yoga altogether. Having different interests give partners some "me time" to enjoy doing the things they like.

2. Secondly, having different interests also means that you will constantly be learning something new about your partner and their hobbies. For instance, suppose your partner loves video games and you are someone who had never played one before. After

some time, whether you like it or not, you will know the names of all the characters, the games, and the difference between a PS3 and PS4. The point being, it expands your knowledge and keeps the relationship interesting as there is always something new to learn and find out about your partner.

3. Thirdly, when you two spend your free time doing something you like such as you go out to meet your friends and your partner goes on to meet the family, the separation will make you miss them and the reunion will be a joyous one. This kind of therapy is also used for couples who fight a lot. A little time alone, and they both start to see things from a different perspective and, more importantly, realize how much they miss their partner.

4. You won't ever run out of things to talk about. Another common objection amongst couples is that they have nothing to talk about. Luckily, when you two have different interests and hobbies, chances are you two will always be conversing about something, even if one partner nearly dozes out during half of it. We have already discussed it several times how crucial communication is.

That being said, we clearly see that having no common interests isn't that big a deal. Of course, it would be ideal to fall in love with someone who is exactly like you, but tell us this: Would you date another you?

So you see, having no mutual interests isn't the biggest problem, not being able to accept the other person's opinion and views is. How many times has it happened that your partner forced you to go jogging with her or join the gym but you would rather spend that time on the couch and watch TV? It is more about acceptance and letting go of trying to fix someone just the way you want them to be.

If that is something you have been trying to do, i.e., imposing your views and interests on them, then there is little hope for you to go forward from here. You must accept the fact that they are different from you and can't be placed in a mold of perfection you concocted in your mind.

WHAT CONCERNS DO YOU HAVE?

One of the many reasons couples fail to reach the common and joyous ground is because deep down they battle many concerns they have regarding their partners. Concerns big enough to start a fight over. Concerns that keeps one doubting the future together. Concerns that are more than just a routine but a habit hard to let go. In this section, we shall look at some of the most common concerns partners in a relationship can have and later learn how active listening and communication can help overcome them once and for all.

1.   Financial

A lot of couples despise the handling of money between them. Life is already so stressful these days and money matters just add to it. Throw in that combo a relationship and you are all in for a rollercoaster ride. The truth is money can be a very touchy subject to converse on.

Some partners don't feel like they are contributing enough, and the conversation just piles onto that guilt of not being able to help out financially. Secondly, there is a budget that needs maintaining and whenever anything goes beyond the decided number, it becomes a concerning worry between the partners. In addition to that, men tend to have this habit of hiding their payrolls and rarely discussing it. Luckily, we are moving past that and each of the partners is contributing equally to make both ends meet.

2.   Mismatched Libidos

We often assume that couples we see holding hands must be rocking the sheets at home. This is far from the truth. In fact, low sex drive, insufficient frequency of sex, or low libidos from either of the partners is a big concern, says Jonathan Bennett, the man behind ThePopularMan.com and also a certified marriage counselor.

According to him, the majority of the couples who come in for counseling are unsatisfied with their sex lives. Some want more of it while others complain of it being too much from one partner's end. Some go through a dry spell for days while others just never initiate the idea of getting hot under the sheets.

It's normal for that spark to phase out after a while. After all, anything new loses its shine upon use. Don't we just put away a toy once we are done playing with it, no matter how many tantrums we threw before to get it? So, it's human nature. But the adventure can always return as long as you are open to different ideas and trying new positions to create excitement.

3.   Lack of Support

Again, this is similar to what we have seen above. Sometimes, we feel unappreciated for all that we do. The lack of appreciation can make one lose interest over time and look for other people for support. The lack of support can also mean an underlying resentment or feelings of supremacy where your partner thinks they do more than you. We all have seen chick flicks and TV shows where one parent fights the other for not doing enough. Appreciation and support is an essential commitment in any relationship. Even an employee that feels unappreciated takes no time resigning, so why should a partner be expected to stay?

4.   Spending Habits

A lot of times, the real issue isn't the paying of bills or saving up for retirement, it's the spending habits your partner has that keeps you awake at night. It usually comes down to the values they have been people have been brought up with. For instance, in some families, it is okay to help out a sibling or parent financially without expecting them to pay it back. Some men and women also have this habit of lending money to friends without an expiration date. Some have this habit of spending it on unnecessary things like partying, clothing, or shoes. If you are worried that your partner is being careless about how they are spending their salary, it is always good to sit them down and have a chat about it.

5.   Boredom

Boredom is bound to settle in after some time, and it isn't even that bad a thing. Even the best friends sometimes feel stuck in a rut. If you feel that though you are together, not really together like old times, it can be a little concerning. It shouldn't last long though. If you feel like the fire is fizzling out and the things you two previously enjoyed indulging in together are just becoming monotonous, they change your methods. Reignite the fire with something different and new. There is always so much you two can try out together from visiting new places to picking up new hobbies.

6.   Jealousy and Possessiveness

It is okay for partners to feel a little jealousy, but there should be a limit to it. There are things called personal space and privacy, and if you feel that your partner constantly invades that, then it is a genuine concern that stems from a lack of trust. As humans, we have always felt insecure about our things – be it toys, people, or habits. This leads to us feeling moderate bouts of jealousy. However, if your partner is on your nerves 24/7, asking who you are with or what you are doing, then it is borderline worrisome. A detailed conversation about why they feel that way and why they feel the separation anxiety when you aren't there is a good way to resolve this issue. The more you talk about it, the better you will understand why they feel insecure about you and if they need to see someone about it.

7.   Extended Family

Even if you collide into each other's families like one, there are always times when they become the cause of a fight between you two. Where will be spending Christmas Eve, who we shall go to visit this year during the Holidays, or why is one family always calling, texting, and coming over? If there is an unspoken battle between the wife and the mother-in-law or a partner and their father, it can become concerning. Why? Because it gets the two of you riled up in a fight and upsets the atmosphere in the house. Don't let outsiders cause a rift between you and always share opinions in a calm and composed manner. The other person shouldn't feel like their family is being insulted and neither should you try to deliberately create a drama.

8.   Cheating and Infidelity

Cheating or infidelity, in most cases, is a hard crime to forgive. Even after multiple counseling sessions, some partners are just never able to forgive. It takes an obscene amount of willingness and honesty to rebuild a relationship after that. Even there, there is always the fear of it happening all over again and you can't seem to find anything the cheating partner does genuine. If a partner has committed infidelity and you aren't able to forgive and forget, it is quite concerning. Trust becomes a major issue that one can't seem to look past. However, it is something that can be worked upon if both parties are willing to admit and forgive.

9.   Kids or No Kids

This is a crucial concern and point of debate among couples or people in a relationship. Some people are wired differently. They come from a big family of siblings and cousins which makes them want some of their own one days too. Conversely, the other partner may not think so because they come from an unloved or conservative childhood where love rarely blossomed. Thus, their point of view is also understandable for not wanting a family of their own.

These concerns should be addressed before getting into a relationship as this isn't something that can be agreed or disagreed upon in case one of the partners isn't up for it. You may find it difficult to cordially end it right now, but it is for the best, as ten years down the lane when the bills start to pile up and the relationship seems like a lot of work, this will eventually bug you.

10.   Falling Out of Love

Last but certainly not least, some partners may also experience falling out of love. The things that were just mere annoyance to you may start to become an unforgettable one. Their flaws may outweigh their aptness. You seem least interested in having a conversation, getting intimate, or just spending time with them. That is you falling out of love.

Some couples that experience this never grow back, but there are ways to rekindle the love. It isn't the end for them. They just need to find their way back and relearn things about their partners.

LISTEN TO WHAT I HAVE TO SAY!

Your body language and actions are what make the relationship beautiful in the beginning. However, with time, when the physical attraction starts to fade away, communicating and active listening become the two most important aspects of it. Although, they don't guarantee a happily ever after, they do help couples to avoid misunderstandings, arguments, fights, and doubts – all of which are ingredients for the perfect recipe for happiness and prosperity in marriage. Poor listening skills can upset a partner even more as they might think that they are being ridiculed, uncared for, or misjudged completely. Therefore, before we head onto the next chapter, we want you to look at some tips to become an effective listener and develop a deeper and nourishing bond with your partner.

- Be patient when you are listening. As humans, our ability to listen is faster than the speed of someone's speaking, which means we might keep interrupting them with our questions even before they are done speaking. Don't do that as it will only disrupt the flow of conversation and break its tempo. Instead of continuing with the story, your partner might have to answer your questions and feel rushed.

- Withhold any judgments you might have and also try to mask your "Oh darling, didn't I tell you so..." expressions as well. If someone is opening up to you, try to mimic the same and be there for them instead of speaking your mind or sharing opinions.

- Be interested in what they are saying; as clearly, it is the most important thing to them. You don't want to be caught trying to pretend to listen or else it would make them feel unvalued or unimportant. Ask for clarification in case you don't understand something as it will mean that you are genuinely interested. The need for clarification can help you concoct a better answer to their queries when they ask for it.

- When probing questions, let them be open-ended. Open-ended questions encourage the speaker to be more comfortable. Asking questions with a yes or no answer can end the conversation sooner.

- Try to make eye contact 60 to 70% of the time. Eye contact is a non-verbal but effective tool to reassure the speaker that you are 100% on board with what they are saying. It also shows your keen interest in the conversation. To further make the conversation more open and verbal, lean towards them and occasionally place your hand onto theirs or hold it if they are about to breakdown. Nod your head occasionally as well. If in a sitting position, avoid folding your arms too.

- Avoid changing the subject abruptly. This can make your partner think that you weren't attentive.

- Use paraphrasing to your advantage. Your partner doesn't necessarily need your advice or opinion. So don't offer it. Period.

- As stated before, keep interruptions from your end to a minimum. They are probably speaking in a flow, straight from their heart. They don't wish to be stopped in between every few minutes just so that you can have everything cleared and understood on your end.

- Furthermore, don't prepare replies in advance or make the mistake of speaking them out. It might change the whole context of what they were about to say. They may seem judged if it were the opposite of what they had in mind.

- Finally, try to be present physically as well as mentally. Our minds can easily wander off or start daydreaming when we are just made to sit and listen to something. It happens with everyone. Remember how in class you would start to daydream and go into another dimension instead of listening to a lecture? This happens because our mind always wants to be the center of attention, and when it isn't, it starts to daydream on its own. Since this is a similar case where you just have to listen without offering any feedback, it will be hard to keep your mind from wandering off. But try to, as it can mean the world to your partner.

CHAPTER - 2
RESOLVING AND PREVENTING CONFLICTS

AND ARGUMENTSLEND ME YOUR EAR

Conflicts and arguments are a normal aspect of relationships. Sometimes, it is these fights that help the couple come closer and understand each other's needs on a deeper level. However, the same fights and arguments can become the reason for separation and even divorce.

In this chapter, we shall take a look at why couples fight, what causes these fights, how they can be prevented, and how to settle down with some workable tips so that couples who keep fighting all the time can take a little break. Moreover, we shall also discuss what kind of fights are beneficial, what you should never do between a mid-fight, and what to do if it gets out of hand.

But before we do all that, let's learn why people fight and what things do they fight about when they are in a relationship together.

WHY ARE WE FIGHTING ALL THE TIME?

Whenever we find ourselves in the middle of a fight, after it has ended or been postponed for a later time, we often wonder what started it. Just a few hours ago, we were this happy couple who no one would think can stay apart for a minute, and now we don't want to see each other's faces even. Perhaps it was something that your partner said or did that pushed the buttons. Or maybe they triggered something within you like a bad memory or thought that just angered you.

Fighting with a partner seems so easy. Sometimes, as natural as talking or laughing together over something silly. After all, they are the closest ones to us. Naturally, we always walk up to them to share our deepest secrets and feelings. They are the closest we have to a family.

Let's get one thing straight first. EVERY COUPLE FIGHTS – even those who say they don't. If you think that you are dealing with the toughest and most arrogant of partners who hurt you by saying the meanest things to you during a fight, you are not alone. Every partner thinks they are living with one or, worse, are that partner themselves. Fighting is a sign of being a typical couple and to just take away the feelings of guilt and regret away from you, let's put all the blame on your brain, shall we?

Jokes apart, it is your brain that deserves all the blame. Here's how!

The brain of every human is wired for war and not love. It is their primary instinct to react with aggression or use their hands to protect themselves against violence and signs of danger. This means that fighting is a fairly natural response if you feel threatened by the harsh words from your partner. Your brain was developed to react to situations that posed danger, thus making them bad at romance and love. So now you get why they always tell you to listen to your heart or think from your heart and not your brain when making decisions about love.

This is all discussed in great length in Stan Tatkin's book called, Wired for Love: How Understanding Your Partner's Brain and Attachment Style Can Help You Defuse Conflict and Build a Secure Relationship (Tatkin, 2012).

He thinks that to understand and improve our marital as well as dating relationships, it is imperative that we first understand the working of the human mind. Our brain is exceptional at picking up signs of danger. It is all just acting and far from the reality that they show in movies, where when one perceives a threat, they become intrigued and let themselves fall into the trap. No such thing will ever happen in reality because, deep down, we are all afraid.

Putting this in the context of a romantic partnership, the threat cues can be as novice as an eye roll, the body language, or the grating tone in their voice. The pissed attitude is perceived as dangerous and thus puts the brain into an enemy mode by triggering the fight or flight response.

The parts that trigger the threat response are called Primitives by Tatkin. Primitives are wired for war, survival-focused, and quick responders in front of potential dangers. Primitives include the following:

- Hypothalamus: Signals the body to freeze, fight or fly.

- Amygdalae: Receives the threat signals brewing in the brain.

- Adrenal and pituitary glands: Release cortisol – the stress chemicals.

Your primitives are least concerned with your happiness or that of your partners. They are also not concerned with the impact your words or actions will have on your partner. The only focus is your survival and victory against whatever threat lies ahead.

Although your partner's grating tone isn't as threatening or dangerous as finding yourself in an underwater cage surrounded by hungry sharks, your brain thinks of both the situations as the same.

When we fight with a partner, rejection or abandonment also serves as threats, which is why we try to avoid them at best. However, sometimes the mind just flips out and results in the fighting.

Now that we understand how our mind perceives fighting, it is only fair that we acknowledge the reasons most couples fight about so that an argument can be prevented before it even begins. Below are ten of the most common reasons for fights between married and unmarried couples. Let's discuss these in detail and also see how you can gracefully counter them instead of jumping right into it with the same passion as your partner's.

1.   Money

Fighting over money is very common among couples. Some fights are on how a partner spends too much on something or about how one should save up. Invest it, lock it up in a bank, or buy ourselves a vacation. The options are endless, but opinions may collide. Sometimes partners also have the habit of judging one another over the choices they make. Did you buy $50 worth of imported coffee beans? You should have tipped the waiter more. We must get new flooring as soon as our paychecks roll in. No, we need to get the leaky pipes fixed first...

And then, there are also fights over whether one should have a joint account or not and how to create a monthly or weekly budget.

Solution: Take a deep breath, sit down, and talk about it. Take out a few hours from the weekend and discuss at great length what needs to be done and how. Write down all these expenses made in the week both big and small to set a weekly budget. Once you have everything sorted out, make it a practice to live by it. Going overboard a little is acceptable but try to remain without the boundaries. At the same time, have an emergency budget as well, just in case. Every time you save some cash from the weekly budget, you can add to the emergency budget or treat yourself with a dinner date.

2.   Kids

Children are another common topic over which couples can start fighting. It can be about how they should be raised, their expenses, spending quality time with them, or helping them out with their homework, etc. Some partners want to raise their children in a specific way. Often parents from different religions or backgrounds fight over how they should be raised, which religion they should follow, which values and traditions they should hold dear and so on and so on.

Again, you first need to sit down and ponder over this deeply. The kids are the ones who will be most affected by the fights you have over them. You love them and therefore want the best for them. But at the end of the day, you need to understand that no matter how much you want to control their lives, they will eventually choose their path. That being said, you should mutually lay some ground rules for them to abide by so that they grow up to be sensible and responsible adults.

3.   Time

Not spending enough time at home or with your partner is another major cause of a fight. You are always busy at the office. You never go out with me anywhere. You are always on your phone when you come home. We never do anything together.

All of these are complaints one partner may have with the other which can easily start a fight. In almost all relationships, there is one person who wants to spend time with their partner and when they feel that their partner lacks a similar interest in them, it can lead to frustration. Thoughts like, "He/she doesn't like me anymore," can stir in one's mind, adding to the aggravation.

Some fights can also be about how partners choose to spend their time together. One partner might want to go for a movie whereas the other partner might want to go to the game. One might want to go hiking whereas others might want to go spend the weekend with their family.

Instead of fighting over how you two want to spend 24 hours of the day, join forces and dedicate a "together time" for every day or the weekend. The goal shouldn't be to prioritize one's interests over the others but rather finding a middle ground. Do things you both enjoy doing, such as partying or going out for dinners.

4.   Priorities

You never give me time. You are always busy on the phone. You are always going out with your friends but you never take me or the kids out.

There are times when partners may start to think that they are no longer a priority in the lives of their spouses. There are no flowers anymore, no unexpected hugs or kisses, or demand for intimacy in the middle of the night.

Priorities change over time and you need to understand that. Your partner may be working extra hard just so that they can provide for the family better. Their priority may no longer be just you. So instead of fighting over it, talk it out. Let them know that you miss the old times and how you two should try to at least spend some time together. Also, make it a rule to limit the use of phones when home so that the two of you can connect.

5.   Sex

There was a time when you just couldn't have enough of it, what changed? Why are you no longer interested in having sex? Is there someone else? Do you not feel attracted to me anymore?

The lack of sex or less of it can easily trigger an argument or fight amongst couples. Since everyone has a different need and libido for sexual intimacy, you might feel left out if your partner rarely initiates it. Perhaps, they are too tired and just want to get to bed. Perhaps, there is so much going on in their heads that sex doesn't find a spot. Perhaps, they think that you no longer enjoy it or sex has become boring for you. There are a dozen reasons why sex can lead to fights, arguments, and even separation.

Thus, understand each other's needs for intimacy and try to meet halfway. Also, instead of being quiet about your needs and wants, openly express your concerns regarding the lack of intimacy and how it is affecting your mental state.

6.   The Past

You haven't forgotten about her, have you? You still are in love with your ex. Why do you keep comparing me with your ex in everything?

The past has a way of creeping up in conversations, especially when the relationship lasted for years. The reason most partners are unable to forget about their exes is that their inclusion became a habit. They started doing things a certain way and still haven't given up those habits and thus the taunting. It is very easy to find yourself in a position where you keep comparing your partner with an ex or thinking that your partner does. But it could all be in your head too.

A lot of times, this thought can be very damaging when it is you that keeps comparing yourself with your significant other's ex. The more you nag about it, the more it will frustrate your partner. If the past, in any way, hurt your partner, it is best to not bring it up in a fight and you will only be hurting them on a deeper level. You two must, at all times, maintain a certain respect for each other's privacy, emotions, and past and not let it get between you two and cause a rift.

7.   Chores

You still haven't fixed the dishwasher; how many times do I have to remind you? Why is there an empty carton of milk in the refrigerator? You could have at least taken out the trash. Why is everything my job?

Chores can trigger fights. Imagine you had a tough day at work and tired to the bone only to come home and see that the kids are still awake, dishes are still sitting in the sink, and your partner is carelessly watching the news while drinking a beer, that too without placing a coaster on the coffee table like you reminded him a thousand times. Wouldn't that majorly piss you off and anger you to the point where you just want to punch their face?

Your partner may have a different concept of cleanliness than you. You need to accept that. Hair in the bathtub or the sink may not drive them crazy or they choose to let go of it. On the other hand, you might find it annoying if they drink right from the carton or forget to place the newspapers where the other stack is every day.

If you sense that your partner isn't too enthusiastic about certain chores like taking out the trash or putting the kids to bed, ask them to help you in some other way. Divide the chores accordingly so that peace can be restored in the house.

WAIT...ARE YOU SAYING FIGHTING IS HEALTHY?

It's not something you would have written in your vows or something that you put up on a Valentine's Day card, but research suggests that fighting between couples is, in fact, quite healthy.

Couples who fight together, stay together, says Joseph Grenny, the man who co-authored the bestseller Crucial Conversations (Petterson & Grenny, 2011). According to him, couples fight rather than sweeping their feelings and emotions under the rug every time they feel insulted, frustrated, and unwanted. This isn't just some random fact but the result of an actual survey conducted during the research for the book involving 1,000 adults. Grenny believes that every time we choose to remain quiet and not express our emotions, we are deliberately avoiding a conflict that can be resolved and thus prevent further hurt. To him, the biggest mistake partners make in any relationship is to avoid arguing. This makes the other partner think that things are okay when they aren't, until one day, you finally explode and bring along luggage worth of fights from the past.

Some couples don't fight because they fear it would cause them to hate each other. They think that the risks of speaking up would only lead to disrupting the peace of the house and their relationship, so they remain quiet and accept things as fate. However, what we fail to take into account is the danger of not speaking up and how it would mess up the relationship ultimately. A lack of communication is a basic reason for failed relationships. Speaking your mind, even if it comes in the form of an argument is beneficial to help you two overcome the differences of ideas, opinions, and thoughts. Not addressing the elephant in the room and pretending that everything is fine will impact your intimacy and trust in your partner.

The survey also listed the top three things couples fight about or, at least, wish to have a decent conversation about but they rarely do – money, sex, and pet peeves.

So discussing the underlying issues is the way to a happier and more fulfilling life with a partner. When sensitive issues are discussed rather than fought about later, it gives both partners peace of mind and helps them grow as a couple together. The act of fighting can also make one realize the importance of the partner's feelings and avoid hurting them again by repeating the mistake made.

THE 4 GOOD FIGHTS!

Not every argument means that it's time to head for the door. Arguments can be settled with some pondering and analyzing what led to it in the first place. As soon as you identify the mistake, you will try your best to avoid it. Because let's face it, fighting hurts. Although no couple would deliberately like to go at it, sometimes, fighting can be good for your relationship. In this section, we shall take a look at occasions when fighting allows us to comprehend our partner's feelings and establish a stronger connection than before.

Surprising, no?

Take a look at these six types of fighting that help rekindle the fizzled love and respect you craved from your partner.

Fights That Spark Awesome Makeup Sex

We have seen it in some of our most favorite rom coms and wished it would happen with us. Remember Mr. and Mrs. Smith, anyone? Did that makeup sex scene after that home-shattering fight not have you wishing you had something this passionate with your partner once? The reason makeup sex is so awesome and passionate is that the partners still possess the same energy and fire that they emitted from within themselves during the argument. So you can expect the same passion under the sheets.

So remember, not every fight has to have a bad ending, some just tend to have a sexier ending as well.

A Fight That Resets Boundaries

Sometimes, we end up crossing a line that we shouldn't have during an argument. It can be something you said that hurt your partner on a deeper level and instantly you regretted saying it. It can be a harsh reminder of their failure, their poor sexual performance, or just a direct hit to their character that catches them off guard and ends up hurting them. That very instant when this realization hits you is the moment you understand how it must be like to be in your partner's shoes right now. Had you two not been arguing, you would have never known the extent of how much your words can hurt your partner and also help you realize a mistake that you don't want to be repeating anytime soon!

Fight Where You Promise to Treat One Another Better

Ever argued so intense that you both regret? Was it hard to move past that and look at each other in the eye again? Many couples, after a fight, realize how damaging it was for their relationship and swear to treat each other better the next time around. The kind of fight that almost turned physical or meant the end of your relationship. Some fights just go to a point where the couple finally concludes that something major needs to

43

be done here to fix it. These kinds of fights are the best because they make you realize that you didn't take into consideration the feelings of your spouse and thus vow to treat them better.

Fight Where You Two Learn Something About Each Other

If you listen carefully, an argument with a partner can be a great source of new information for you. Thus, use your mind when listening to what they say. Perhaps they felt hurt over a random joke you made. Since you wouldn't want them to feel insulted or humiliated, your goal will be to avoid repeating the same. But how did you learn about it? During a fight, right? So, in a way, arguments can help the two of you to understand each other better.

WHEN IS FIGHTING NOT THE ANSWER!

Fighting isn't okay when it turns into something more than just an argument. For instance, if your words start to change the meaning or hit more personally, then it just means that you are hitting below the belt which you shouldn't. It is okay to say that you are disappointed with your partner because they didn't go something they were told to but a completely different thing to call them a lazy slob and regret why you ever married them in the first place. I hope you see the difference between the two.

According to Gilda Carla, a relationship expert, Ph.D., marriage counselor, and the author of Don't Lie on Your Back for a Guy Who Doesn't Have Yours, suggests that arguments that start with the word "you" are more damaging because "you" in a fight is synonymous to pointing fingers (Carla, 2017). The partner is left with nothing but to come back at it with an attack. And before we realize, the sanctity of the relationship is broken, no one wants to hear the other, disrespect runs rampant, and the issue at hand goes unresolved.

So what should a healthy fight look like? One where there is respect for the other, one where issues are resolved calmly and maturely and where words are used with care.

If the fighting looks like any of the examples given below, then it has turned into something uglier and both you need to rethink where you two are coming from and what underlying issues are resulting in the fights.

A Fight Where You Are Keener About Being Right

Sometimes, an argument isn't about an issue but rather about one partner trying to be right about something. Didn't I tell you so, but jeez, do you ever listen to me?

When a fight turns from an argument to who was right, things get messy. But ask yourself this, would you rather be right about something or be happy with your significant other? If winning triumphs your thoughts, then the problem lies with you and not them. Your sole goal has become to put down your partner and make them realize that they were wrong instead of settling it. Try to let go when fighting over little things and make efforts to work it out maturely and sensibly instead of pulling your partner's leg.

45

You Keep Fighting Over the Same Issues

A lot of times we don't realize that the reason we have started to fight daily over petty things is an underlying issue that needs to be resolved. Even the tiniest of things your partner does start to annoy you and initiates an eye roll, physical distance, or a sarcastic or agitated tone. These underlying issues must be addressed at the earliest because no one likes to fight over something insignificant and that too, every other day. Thus, if you think that the reason anything your partner does annoys you, find out what could be bothering you.

The Fight Is About Your Partner's Lifestyle Choices

Imagine an argument where you keep reminding your partner how boring they are as they don't like to party like you do over the weekends and instead choose to stay at home and watch some shows on Netflix. First things first, this is something you already knew about your partner when you met them. So you have no right to fight about how they choose to spend their weekend. Secondly, when you fight over it, you are just hitting them below the belt by suggesting that their life isn't as exciting or fun. No partner in a committed relationship should have to change for the other unless for the better. We all have personal preferences, and if he/she isn't stopping you from going out and partying like it's 1999, then you have no right to ask them to give up their leisure activity. Your partner may start to think that they aren't good enough for you or make you happy even though they shouldn't be guilty of them.

46

Instead of fighting about it, choose to compromise and meet each other halfway. If your partner isn't expecting you to stay home with them, you shouldn't force them to go out and vice versa.

A Partner Uses the Argument to Personally Criticize the Other

All you wanted to say was, honey, can you please take out the trash or honey, how long before the dinner is served. But instead, here's what you said.

Why can't you take out the trash yourself? Why do I have to remind you every day? At least, be responsible for once, or Jeez, why are you so slow? How long does it take to prepare a meal? Why are you so lazy?

What you did there is more than just taking out your anger. You chose to personally attack them. When your words and actions hit one's character, it can create a divide between you two. Attacking someone's personality will only leave them to feel animosity towards you because they will feel insulted and humiliated. And if it comes out in front of friends or family, you can expect a fight as soon as they are out of the door. Therefore, be careful with how you choose to express your anger. No partner needs to feel unworthy.

The Fight Is About Not Arguing at All

Some couples fight over the fact that they don't fight over anything. Yes, ironic, I know, but this is one of the most common reasons for fights. When there aren't fights or arguments between couples, it means that feelings aren't communicated as they should be and that lack of communication only adds to the frustration levels and results in a distance between them. A partner may think that the reason the other partner doesn't fight is that they no longer care about it anymore and that emotional detachment can mean a hundred different things. Recall the time when you two first met. Did your partner not like hearing your point of view or present her case and opinions? Now imagine, you stopped doing all that. What kind of message should your partner get from that? The most common reaction would be that you don't care about anything anymore. When issues aren't discussed between partners or worse, discussed with someone else, they can fester inner conflict and make you less happy. Keep in mind that avoidance can mean a dead relationship.

The Fight Is About the Way You Fight

The majority of our fights begin with less important issues. However, when one of the partners starts to yell or point fingers, the fight no longer remains about that issue anymore. The argument shifts from that to how one fights and loses all patients or raises their voice. This only escalates the fight to a point where both the partners feel emotionally hurt by the way their opinion was heard and received.

Five Things You Should Never Do Mid-Fight

There are two ways to fight with a partner. The first is
a productive and respectful way where you don't go after one another like animals and respect each other's

personal space. And then there is the unproductive or toxic way that includes yelling, pushing, verbal accusing, and a lot of judgment and cursing. It is important to note that during any fight, no matter how big or small, emotional or physical abuse should never be the mode. Where abuse becomes the norm and one partner fears the other, it becomes violence. No couple, in their sane minds, should even go there.

That being said, there are several things we do that just makes the argument a whole lot worse. It can be our harsh or sarcastic comments that just flip off a partner or our unintentional actions like punching the table or throwing or breaking things. Therefore, it is always helpful to take note of the things you might do to your partner that would historically mark it as the worst fight you two had. In this section, we are going to discuss 5 things you could do that would piss off a partner like anything and not end well. Avoid these and you two can act like adults and resolve the issue with a less heated up fiasco.

You Go Overboard with Insults

It is never acceptable to name call or prey on someone's insecurities or vulnerabilities when arguing with them. You may be frustrated and angered with the way they are handling it, but that still doesn't give you any right to hit below the belt or call them names. It is very easy for some partners to use insults to belittle their opponent and since they have been together for a long time and are aware of their partner's weaknesses and insecurities, they think that by doing so, it will give them an upper hand and prove them right. Sadly, it does the exact opposite and shows how insensitive you are and how low you can go to prove that you are right.

The biggest issue with personal attacks is that the partner may never forget and forgive that, and it will become difficult to see past that no matter how many times the other partner apologies. Therefore, it is best to avoid any sort of personal attacking just to prove your point and focus solely on the issue at hand rather than beating about the bush and hurting your partner where it hurts the most. The element of respect should never be violated mid-fighting and both the partners should know that.

You Take a Major Decision During the Fight

When things get heated, couples say things they usually end up regretting. When one is in an argument, they are not in the right mind to make sane decisions and therefore should avoid doing so. Unless they have done something unforgivable, wait for things to cool down before you reach a decision.

You Walk Away During the Fight

Referred to as stonewalling, it is when one partner shuts down the other one completely and disengages himself/ herself from the situation during an argument. Not only is that disrespectful, but it also ends the argument in the middle without any plausible conclusion. It can also augment your partner's anger and rage. If the reason you walked out is that you needed some air or a timeout to think things through or to stop yourself from doing something horrendous, then clearly voice your concern for bailing out. Let them know that you have heard where they are coming from and will think about what has been said. This is a more dignified way of handling any argument mid-fight, which prevents heartache and detachment among couples.

Your Body Language Is Misleading and Judgmental

Most of the time, we are so focused on the fight and what the other partner is saying that we fail to sense the responses of our body towards those words. Non-verbal actions speak your true mind because they can't be faked in moments like these. So if your partner catches you rolling your eyes over some suggestions they just made, it probably tells them that you don't see it as a smart one and are, in reality, just mocking them. Would it be wrong if they feel more aggravated then? Because clearly, you are saying something and doing something else. How are they to trust your words and not your actions? Feelings depicted during a fight usually come accompanied by big energy. For instance, if you are angry over something, it is quite natural to use hand gestures to portray that. You might unintentionally push your partner without thinking because that is your way of lashing out. You are probably going to regret it later, but it might not be something forgivable in the eyes of your partner.

So, be sure to fight mindfully and limit energy. No need

to get hyped up during a fight when later, you two are probably going to resolve it in a calm and relaxed manner.

You Keep Bringing Up Past Mistakes

Sorry to be pointing fingers, but women do tend to bring up things quite unrelated to an argument, making it irrelevant. I am positive not all ladies do that and not all guys are perfect, but bringing up past laundry to a present argument and expecting your partner to feel guilty over it is no way to resolve a fight. The moment you bring up any unresolved grievances to the table, the present issue no longer remains the main issue, and you two are back to square one. You start fighting over something you fought over before as well, but there was no resolution to that. So what if a partner cheated in the past? No need to keep reminding them about it over and over again, especially when they sincerely apologized. Making that the only definition of who they are (a cheater) you may win the argument, but you may end up hurting your partner more.

This isn't how you fight fair, especially with a partner who is already thin-skinned and guilt-ridden about it. It will only make the fight more contentious and counterproductive. Worse of all, your partner may become extra defensive. If you still have some unresolved grievances towards your partner, set a time to discuss that at some other date. But don't keep bringing it up every time you think you are going to lose.

I Don't Want to Fight Anymore

Regardless of all that we have discussed earlier, the truth remains the same. No couple enjoys fighting. Even when they do fight, they want to end it as soon as possible. There are several ways to settle an argument. Ways that will not only help you as a couple goes back to how you were but also allow you to grasp the reasons why it happened and how to prevent it in the future.

Under this section, we shall talk about how to restore balance in the relationship after an argument. After all, for how many days do you expect to ignore each other? You will eventually have to get back together.

How to Restore Balance in a Relationship

Resolving an argument with your significant other? Is that even possible? Won't they just keep bringing it up from time to time? Have you ever met my spouse?

Well, the truth of the matter is that settling an argument is fairly easy when both the partners acknowledge the differences in opinions and are ready to address the issues decently. We shall discuss more on this in Part 3, but for now, let's learn some foolproof means to not only end an argument but settle it once and for all.

Focus on the Present

Arguments are the result of unsettled conflicts from the past. However, trying to bring up something entirely different from what you two are fighting about will only add to the resentment you two have. Avoid doing that and focus on the current issue only. This also goes for all those times when you try to use that past to prove a point or convey a message. If anything, it can make your partner feel attacked or judged and shift attention from the present issue.

However, if you keep finding yourself bringing past grievances, it means you still aren't over them and to move forward, you must sit down and resolve them first.

Personalize Your Statements with "I"

Use sentences that emphasize more on a personalized experience rather than a general one. For instance, if you felt insulted when your partner joked about your weight in front of his friends, instead of saying something like, it's disrespectful when you joke about my weight with our guests," say something like, "I felt so disrespected when you joked about my weight in front of your friends. I felt humiliated. "

Which of the statements has a deeper impact and yet gracefully delivers the message across? Statements starting with a personalized note, like the word "I," allow your partner to see how hurt you felt.

Avoid Being Passive-Aggressive

Next, try not to act passive-aggressive. This won't help settle any argument – big or small. Passive-aggressive behaviors are poison for communications and only make arguments worse. Instead of expressing your anger with words, you choose behaviors like trying to make one jealous, gossip, pretend they don't exist, or cease communicating with them at all. Always choose to speak your mind so that the issue may get resolved as soon as possible without escalating to something bigger. A lot of partners choose to stay quiet or use a sarcastic tone instead of just saying, "I am mad at you," thus leaving their partners in a mix of confusion and cluelessness as to how to move past this silence.

As stated above, use "I" statements to let your partner know that you have done something to upset them instead of hiding from them or ignoring them. The more open you are, the easier it will become to settle an argument.

Use Suitable Language

Never use derogatory language during an argument as it will do anything but settle it. The words you choose and the way you deliver them is very important in any fight with your partner. You may have a different body language that counters your words. Even when you are in a heated conversation, use appropriate language to express your emotions. You have to stay respectful and ensure that your partner doesn't feel disrespected either. This means that you aren't allowed to name call them as labels can sting you back in the ass the next time you fight with them.

Even when you think you will lose your mind if you continue with the debate, choose to refrain from using harsh words or cursing. Yelling is also not acceptable at any cost. The reason you have to be extra special with the tone and pitch of your voice is that sometimes we don't even realize that we are yelling unless the other person points it out. If you are being told to lower your voice down, do that instantaneously.

Openly Communicate Your Expectations

Be clear about what you expect what your partner needs to do. No need to confuse them with riddles or avoid conversing with them just because they did something that you didn't like. Sometimes, our words can also have double meanings or be understood in different manners, which is why it is always best to be crystal clear about your expectations when settling an argument with your partner.

Reach Out for Support

If the issue doesn't reach a fruitful conclusion still, maybe you need someone else to intervene and take over. Sometimes, a new perspective can help both partners see the problem from a completely different angle. This is where professional counseling or therapy comes in. Hire a marriage counselor to improve communication. A professional counselor may help you with tips on how to talk to each other without riling up or how to resolves arguments and conflicts.

CHAPTER - 3

ACCEPTING AND SHARING OPINIONS

Some people, when they start dating, think that having differences in opinions about politics, religion, values, or morality means they will always be fighting over things from day one. This is far from reality and only becomes a problem when both parties refuse to take into account each other's viewpoints. Instead of accepting them or viewing them as a new perspective, they perceive it as something negative and thus, are always trying to change them. Opinions can be changed, but they don't always have to. If we take things back to the day you two met, was it not your differences that attracted you to each other in the first place? There is a strong backing behind opposites attract – proven both by science and psychological experts.

Having a different opinion does indeed complicate things slightly in a relationship but there are many ways to deal with it.

In this chapter, not only shall be looking at these, but we shall also learn about why people have different opinions, why they should be accepted and appreciated.

57

I HAVE SOMETHING TO TELL YOU?

The moment couples start living together, they are bound to come across diverse opinions – most of which may not match yours. This can lead to misunderstandings as well as arguments over even the smallest of issues such as what to dress your kid as on Christmas. If you come from a Jewish family and your partner is a hardcore Christian, this argument may seem quite valid as Christmas isn't a celebrated holiday according to the Jewish tradition. They celebrate Hanukkah instead. The same differences can also be seen in how the money is spent in the house, who gets to make the final call, who gets to discipline the kids, who is responsible for housekeeping and raising the kids, etc.

But where do these differences come from?

For starters, we all come from different households, neighborhoods or different sides of the country. Partners may have been raised in a certain way that conflicts with the other's way of living. In some houses, it is considered bad to talk back to your husband; whereas, in some homes, nearly all the major decisions are taken mutually after thorough discussions. This diversification of environments and early childhood experiences play a crucial role in personality development. Your partner may come from a family that spent every summer vacation out in the woods, but you may have never experienced anything as outdoorsy. Therefore, when it comes to taking the kids to someplace, your partner may insist on renting an RV and heading for the woods while you might be more interested in visiting the entertainment hub of the country for some family time together.

Then, we also have different educations, different exposures, different jobs, and different perspectives about life. All of these can easily become problematic when going unheard or unresolved.

However, these differences don't mean that your partner is right and you aren't or in any way demean you. Accepting others' opinions is a crucial aspect of every marriage. A relationship can be fostered with unity and understanding where every different idea gets discussed with an open mind.

Why You Should Listen to What Your Partner Has to Say

We believe everyone should see the world as we do. We think of it as the right way and are rarely keen on changing our minds about it. When we are paired in a relationship with a partner who has a completely different point of view than yours, it is so easy to blame them for being misinformed or living with a distorted opinion about reality.

But they think the same about your views too. So how to go on living with them when you constantly feel that they are wrong and vice versa?

First off, each individual is entitled to their opinions. Opinions are formed based on real events and make the individual who they are. As we already discussed how different upbringings and household practices and values can be different and thus form their opinion about something, as a couple, those views should always be valued and respected.

They aren't wrong, just different.

When you two are journeying together, keep in mind that it is never going to be easy or simple as a straight line. You both chose to be together and thus must provide each other with some space and understanding about the things they solely believe in. Having a partner with a different opinion is also a healthy thing for many reasons. For starters, it will enrich and broaden your vision about reality. Next, it allows you to question your own beliefs and opinions and see if you are wrong. A different opinion can also give you the chance to ask them what made them think that way or why do they believe what they believe in. The newfound information can help you two understand each other better and strengthen your relationship, as then you will be more considerate when discussing important issues with them.

Thirdly, when you acknowledge and accept your partner's opinions, they will feel more valued and understood. When they feel that, they will be more open with you and feel safe sharing their deepest thoughts and ideas with you without feeling judged. The level of trust between you two will blossom, and your partner won't need to amplify their views just to be heard.

It also helps to bridge the gap between you two as you learn to respect each other's viewpoints. Moreover, there may be times when one of your decisions may require more thinking on your part and your partner may help you see it. For instance, you are thinking to get a new job. You are thinking of a good pay raise and fewer working hours. However, you might overlook aspects like long commute hours and heavy traffic. If your partner knows how frustrated you get when you drive for long hours, they may ask you to reconsider. You might feel a little taken aback by their idea and believe that they don't want to see you succeed. But when you two sit down to discuss why you think it's a great idea and why they think otherwise, a different point of view may change your mind. You may come to realize that their worry wasn't about you earning more but rather about your mood and health. So a different point of view can help you see past all the glittery stuff.

You can also visualize the long-term impacts of your decisions. For instance, if we follow-up with the same example as above, your primary objective was short-term goals. You just wanted to work a few hours less and get paid more. However, your partner's concern was more about your health. Who knows, ten days into the new job and you are back to hating your life again and regretting ever leaving your previous job.

A difference of opinion can also help you overcome your weaknesses. As humans, we have the habit of underestimating our skills and talents. We always think that we aren't good enough. That is your opinion of yourself. Chances are, you may have backed down on some good potential opportunities in the past due to the same fear. Now enter a partner into this situation who thinks no one can beat you at the skill you are good at.

This positive and refreshing boost of an entirely different opinion of yourself will improve your self-confidence.

How to Resolve Contradictory Opinions Without Fighting?

Differing opinions will arise between partners – that's a given! How you are going to resolve them is the more important question. Sometimes, these differences in views can become the reason for fights and arguments between couples. So how can they move past that and accept and respect each other's opinions without breaking into a fight?

We have some great advice to offer. Take a look!

Negotiation

Negotiation or compromise is a suitable way to come out of a difference in opinions during complex situations. When you two want to do something your way and the partner intervenes with their methodologies, opt to compromise. Find a way in which neither one of you feels left out or disrespected. If you two can't reach a consensus and aren't; willing to give up on your stance, it is best to avoid attempting it at all. After all, nothing can be more important than your relationship, right? Don't be hell-bent on proving yourself right all the time.

Don't Argue

Sometimes, it can be very hard to change someone's perspective about things because they are very personal to them. In that case, it is unfair on your part to expect them to give it up. You must understand where they are coming from and why they think a certain way. If no mutual ground can be found, you must retreat.

Be Sensible

What your partner is saying might be rational, and you know it, but if you continue to argue, then that is just egoistic on your part. Try putting yourself in your partner's shoes and look at the world from their eyes for once. If you know that they are right and you keep fighting for the sake of being right, then you need to back up and accept it as a mature individual.

Don't Force It

It is unhealthy to impose your beliefs on someone and expect them to fully abide by them. No one ever said that differences of opinions are a bad thing. Forcing someone to think a certain way because you think it is right isn't justifiable. That would be acting childish. Speak your mind and let the other person decide if they think it is right or not. Don't force it upon them.

Act Mature

Could they be right? If there is the slightest possibility that what your partner is sharing is, in fact, rational, accept it as an adult. Hey, we all can be wrong at times. At least, accepting it will let your partner feel valued and also leave you with some newfound knowledge. You are never too old to learn something new.

CAN I BE A PART OF THIS TOO?

Every second we are making some new decisions. The decision about what we are going to wear today, what would we have for breakfast, whether to stop for coffee on the way or not, whether to respond to emails first, etc. Some decisions don't require much thought. They can be answered with either a yes or no. However, some decisions require thinking and analyzing. Decisions which must first be checked in with the people you are living with. Once you get married, any decision you think requires some comprehension must be run through with your spouse first. Why? Because chances are they will be affected by it too. For example, suppose you decide to go on an all-boys trip with your office mates over the weekend. Just a little camping or fishing trip. You tell your friends to keep their bags packed only to come home to realize that your partner also has something big the same weekend and was hoping that you would want to look after the kids.

You committed the boys without checking it with your wife first and now you are in a dilemma to either lie to her or tell her and hope that she would stay back. Had you just asked her about her plans before saying yes to your friends, you could have avoided the awkwardness and all the lying, right?

So it is only a matter of consultation since marriage is a mutual commitment you two made to each other. Decisions, taken alone, without concerning with a spouse can have detrimental effects on your relationship. Hiding things from them or deliberately not sharing it with them can create distance between you two and affect your emotional, sexual, and mental health.

What Decisions Are Considered Important?

Of course, there are some decisions that you can take on your own, such as getting a haircut or what to wear to a party, there are some decisions that must always be decided upon mutually. Firstly, what you think is worthy of a discussion is the most important decision you need to make. In many households, women often feel left out when their partners take big decisions without their knowledge. Things like investing in property or taking out a big loan. The men assume that women have nothing to do with the knowledge or won't be able to offer any advice in this regard, which is why there is no need to involve them in this.

This could be extremely hurtful in case the partner finds it out from elsewhere. Not only will they feel left out, but they will also think that their partner thinks of them as naïve with zero valuable knowledge. Once it is out in the open, it is likely to turn into an argument where both the partners will feel more hurt. So what other decisions should the couple mutually decide and agree upon from the moment they said their vows to each other?

- Where will you live?
- How will the house be managed?
- How will the chores be divided?
- Who will be in charge of the finances and how will they be managed mutually?

- How will family trips be decided?

- How much time will be spent with the family?

- How will a crisis be handled?

- What will be the plan for retirement and advanced care?

- What parenting style would be ideal?

And that isn't all! Do you also need to discuss what will happen when one partner wishes to change a set decision? For instance, you two decided on a monthly budget. What if one partner wishes to go slightly overboard with it and buy something urgently? Whether to go overboard or wait is also another decision that must be made mutually.

What Things Should Be Mutually Decided?

Although we briefly listed some important things to be decided mutually, there are also some things that partners think they don't need to discuss with their spouses, but they do. Gladly, we have taken it upon us to save you the embarrassment as well as the argument and anger by listing some more things your partner would like to be included in.

Spontaneous Outings

There are two ways of saying a thing. Try to pick the differences between each of these sentences and guess why your spouse might feel mad.

66 "I was thinking about going on a trip for a few days. Work

is just too hectic and I need a break. What do you think about it?"

"Hey, I am going away this weekend to hike."

Do you see the difference? The first one is more of a suggestion and an idea that you are sharing, whereas the second one seems like a decision you already took on your own without consulting your spouse and now just letting them know about it, expecting they will be alright with it.

If you are planning a spontaneous trip without letting your partner, the plan can go wrong in so many ways. Your partner may feel devalued and angry because whenever they ask you to do something, you always make the excuse of not having enough time. They would expect you to complete the pending chores first and then think about a trip. Besides, they might already have plans for the weekend elsewhere and are certainly not happy with the fact that you are just telling them the last minute.

Quitting a Job

You can't just quit your job one day without first consulting with your partner about how the finances will be managed if you quit. Quitting our job is a big decision, even for you. Of course, there are days when frustration would kick in and all your hard work will go unappreciated. But that isn't reason enough to quit, especially when you haven't thought it through. Any decision made in a moment of anger is often a regretful one and you don't want that. The reasons you should discuss this with your partner first is so that they can release some of your tension regarding it, understand where you are coming from and provide some genuine options to opt for instead of just quitting. Your partner might have had planned to move into a bigger space by the end of next year and with your finances out of the equation, it could delay that.

Taking a New Job

Similarly, when you plan on starting to work or change jobs, your partner should be the first one to hear that thought. If you think your spouse is even the tiniest bit wise, chances are their input in your decision to take up a job may be constructive. You don't want to start a new job without evaluating all the pros and cons of it. Luckily, your partner, who holds a different perspective, can help you see them more clearly and help you reach a more sensible decision.

Investing Money

If it's your money and your partner or family has nothing to do with it (such as inheritance), then you may choose to invest it anywhere you like. However, if it affects your lifestyle, education, and upbringing of your kids and your social status, then your spouse must know where it is going and why. Even if it is just sitting idle in a bank, your partner has every right to know where you plan to invest it in case they already had plans for investing it elsewhere.

Changing Religions

This shouldn't be an issue if you are an interfaith couple and wish to practice your separate religions. However, an issue may arise when you two are of the same faiths and one of you decides to change theirs. Moreover, if your partner is extremely religious, it can be a bigger problem. Changing faith isn't as simple as changing cars or houses. Changing your faith affects multiple aspects of your life as a couple such as how will the kids be raised, what religion they follow, how will your social life be, what will be the reaction of the family and even how you vote. Tell us that all these aren't important enough to warrant a discussion in your eyes?

Changing Birth Control

This may come as a surprise, but every couple has a birth plan. Some love surprises that come in the form of cuddly babies, but not all. If you are, for any reason, changing your birth-control prescription, your partner needs to be in on that discussion. If you want to go off the pill due to some health concerns and you still aren't planning a baby for the next year, you need to let your partner know that they should wear a condom or be careful around sex during your fertile window. Moreover, if you are planning to give up the whole idea of parenthood, your partner needs to know that too. Just thinking that they would be okay with it because they hate kids anyways is an estimation and not their final answer. They might not want them now but think about having them later in life.

Taking in a Sibling or Relative

Is a friend of yours going to crash in for a few weeks because her apartment is infested? Is your brother going to be living with us now that he is in town and looking for a job? These are questions that couples need to discuss before inviting the guest into the house. Also, you can't just bring in somebody without asking them how long are they going to stay. Always ask your partner if they would feel comfortable around the new member in the house or not. Of course, there wouldn't be any point asking them in front of the guest, who by the way, has already settled in. Don't give your partner a surprise this big, especially if they aren't extrovert and like to spend their time in the home privately.

Taking Out a Bank Loan

Since you two are tied for eternity or until death do you part, your finances are going to affect your partner's too. Taking out a debt means they will have no option but to pay up in case they fail to. Not doing so could mean losing everything – the house, the car and saved up money. Therefore, discuss it thoroughly with your partner why you are doing this and plan how you are going to return it. Set up an emergency fund in case you get late on a few payments as well. All this is only possible when you have your partner on board through and through. Best of all, what if the money can be arranged from elsewhere without intervention from the bank?

Bringing Home a Pet

Although bringing in a new pet isn't as big as coming home to find a new member in the house, it is still best to consult with your partner or at least let them know beforehand. If the marriage is fairly new and you have little idea about how your partner will react to the fluffy addition, or you don't know of any childhood traumas they have with a pet, it is best to discuss it with them and see if they are okay. After all, on days when you aren't home and they are, it will be their responsibility to look after it. Are they prepared for that? Add to that the trips to vet clinics and the money for procedures that will come out of both of your paychecks.

Buying a Property

Again, it only looks good in movies where the guy buys the girl a big condo away from the suburban with a lake view in the backyard. In reality. There are a dozen things to think about before taking such a big step. One has to think about their job, how long will the commute take, how far would be the kid's school be, how will you meet your family, etc. Decisions this big require that input from both partners is received and the decision to move or not should be mutual. You can't expect your partner to just give up everything and move into the new house – maybe some years down the lane but not right now when they are at the peak of their career or expecting a big promotion.

How to Make Joint Decisions

When you get married, many things change. Marriage is different than dating and involves decisions taken jointly. You are no longer the sole decider in the relationship and have to consult things with your partner. It involves more than just sharing the same space. The moment you get married, you need to start navigating your life forward with your partner by the side.

Decision-making is one of those habits that is hard to give up and often is the reason for conflicts and arguments among couples. Where one partner may think it isn't important enough to garner a discussion, others might think otherwise. Since both the partners come from different backgrounds, it is always difficult to put your heads together and think like one. So to help you see eye-to-eye on things and how to mutually decide things, here are some great tips to make the process of deciding mutually less daunting.

Don't Shut Your Partner Out

A lot of times, we think that our ideas are so brilliant that it doesn't need any more intervention. However, even when you think that it should be discussed with your partner. If they think of it as brilliant too, kudos to you. If they don't, listen to what they have to say before shutting them out completely. You must always know what other options are available and whether they are less risky or not. You mustn't unilaterally say no to whatever they have on their minds as it would only crush their self-esteem. It will also wither their spirits, and they will feel abhorred and left out. If you are going to go with whatever you have decided, at least give them the peace of being heard and politely discard their ideas with valid explanation and why you think they won't work.

Listen to Your Gut

When evaluating different opportunities, pay close attention to what your gut is telling you. Sometimes it happens that even the best of ideas don't feel satisfactory. There is always something bothering you about it. If your partner discussed something important with you and you can't seem to get it out of your head because it feels wrong, let them know. If the thought of it makes you anxious, let them know that too. There might be something you guys missed anticipating and even though you might still struggle to identify the cause of the anxiety, you will still know that it needs more comprehension. A detailed discussion with your partner about it can help you in two ways. First, your partner, with a satisfactory explanation may calm your anxiety. Second, they might also delay taking the decision and ponder over it some more. Intuition is a very strong feeling and mustn't be shunned away as casual doubts. If an upcoming decision bothers you, discuss it and then decide the course of action mutually.

Be Genuine with Your Demands

The goal should be to work diligently so that a sensible and real agreement can be reached upon. There mustn't be any cohesion involved. You have no right to make your partner want the same things by giving them ultimatums. At the same time, you are in no position to change their minds about something using manipulation or other underhanded methods. Forcing someone to do something isn't the same as agreeing. If you wish to strengthen your relationship with your spouse, having an open and respectful conversation is the way to go. If things still don't work out and you two fail to reach mutual accord, then it is best to avoid doing it altogether.

Share your Feelings

Don't fear communication, thinking it would start a fight. If you have a different opinion to present something and think of it as a more sensible one; share it. If you don't converse or share the responsibility of decision-making with your spouse, they might think you are least interested. The next time, they might not even discuss and go behind your back about something involving you. Would you feel good about it, especially if it isn't how you wanted it to be?

Therefore, always share your feelings and express your concerns with your partner, so that later on, you don't resent them for making decisions for you as well.

Be Willing to Compromise

Compromise creates a win-win situation between partners. It prevents the need to shut down one's ideas or thoughts completely and helps the couple use the best of what both minds have conceived individually. Sometimes, it is also okay to just go with what your partner wants without causing a scene. Keep in mind that starting a fight about something is easy but continuing with it and reaching a fruitful conclusion is hard. Therefore, don't create a fuss over every little thing and learn to let go sometimes. Compromising doesn't make you less competent in an individual. There must surely be the thing you do better than your spouse and if they don't interrupt and go along with how you want them to be, try and do the same for them. Losing your grip a little won't cause you any harm.

It is the best way to maintain harmony in your relationship. You two should always try to work as a team but also be willing to bend a little for the other one whenever needed. If your spouse's decisions about something don't cause you any harm, then consider giving it a thumbs up.

CHAPTER - 4

IMPROVING COMMUNICATION

Communication is the most important building block of every relationship. In Parts 1 and 2, we learned how a lack of communication between partners can lead to poor listening as well as arguments and conflicting opinions between partners. We also saw how poor communication between partners can lead to unhappy and unhealthy marriages, something nobody deserves.

Therefore, in this chapter, we are going to be talking about how to improve communication between partners, understand the various barriers in between and see if a handful of interesting activities and exercises can improve it.

DO YOU UNDERSTAND WHAT I AM TRYING TO SAY?

Have you ever seen people play Chinese Whisper (the Telephone Game)? Do you see how poor their guesses are when they try to say the words they thought they heard the other person said? Most of the time, the actual word or sentence gets lost in the transfer and something similar happens in relationships too. When partners don't openly communicate with each other, the feelings, emotions, and happiness get distorted. When most of the things you want to say to them remain in your heart, they just die a terrible death. Therefore, to make your union more meaningful and happy, we must learn of the barriers to communication couples face when trying to converse with others so that your relationship is not like the Chinese Whisper itself.

THE BARRIERS TO COMMUNICATION

Choosing the Wrong Time

Choosing a time when one or both the partners are not emotionally available can be the biggest barrier in between. When trying to have important conversations, always schedule a time for them to be discussed in detail. Additionally, keep in mind that you have to eliminate all external distractions as well which means putting down your phones, turning off the TV, and giving each other full attention. There is no point in having a conversation when both the partners are distracted or have something important going on in their minds. Those types of conversations rarely leave a mark and thus, set time aside for important conversations.

Being Too Judgmental

When listening to what your partner has to say, try not to be judgmental or picky or it will make them feel disrespected. One of you might actually have an important concern to discuss, but judging from the disrespectful attitude, they might decide not to. Therefore, always be open to communicate and listen attentively. Wait until the partner has there turn and then offer something in return. Keep in mind that if they are coming to you for an unbiased opinion, they should get that. If they don't, this will probably be the last time they open up to you. How would you feel if you were in their shoes?

Being Too Critical or Negative

When a partner is being negative about all the ideas you have to present, they will stop coming to you with more as your unsupportive attitude will make them feel less valued. The goal should be to be more expressive and negativity only suppresses one's freedom of speech. Being too critical can also be interpreted as a lack of appreciation from your partner, which will further drive them away from you.

Interrupting Them During the Talk

Sometimes, a partner is only looking for a means to vent out their frustration or grief. They aren't seeking answers and if you happen to offer just that by interrupting them in between, it will make them feel foolish. They too know what they should do, they just want your support, not your opinion or advice. Interruption can also be a barrier to future conversations where the partner feels that they are not given the chance to fully express themselves.

Using "You" Statements

The excess of the word "you" in conversations alienates the speakers from the problem and blames the other partner instead. It becomes more of a back and forth blame game than a healthy conversation. On the other hand, using "I" statements can seem more empathetic and heard. The other partner doesn't feel like they are the only ones with the problem. "I" statements also mean that the partner also shares the blame and is, therefore, open to discussing it.

Signs Your Communication Is Good or Bad

Now that we identified the barrier to communication, we need to test how good or poor it already is so that we can work towards making them more beneficial, result-oriented and fruitful. Think of it as a step-by-step process. The first step to any problem is identification. The second step involves addressing the issues or identifying if the problem actually persists or not. Finally, we will look at the means to resolve it. Since we already discussed the barriers in the section above, the only sensible step is to move towards the second step which involves identifying if the communication is good or not.

Good: Your conversations are deep and meaningful

Whenever you sit down to chat, you create this amazing aura where you two are your true self. You don't have to hide anything about each other or feel less valued. When you talk, you discuss everything from the start of your day to the end of it and everything good or bad in between. You openly talk about prospects and aren't afraid to work towards it. You also are expressive with your emotions and feelings and feel that there is nothing that can come between the two of you.

Bad: Your conversations are bland and non-existent

There is no levity in the conversations you have. You two practically live like two strangers in the same house, having your own interests and hobbies. You don't care about how your partner's day was nor do they ask about it. You may seem like the perfect couple to outsiders but you rarely have those moments where you can freely express yourself in front of them.

Good: You two are attentive listeners

We all need to be heard and if you have someone in your life with attentive ears, you are the luckiest soul on the planet earth. You two are exceptional active listeners and support each other without judgment or biases. You handle each discussion maturely like adults without accusing each other. You offer advice or opinion only when asked for.

Bad: You talk more than you listen

There is more noise than an actual conversation because you two seem to start talking at the same time. None of you are willing to listen and just want to express how you feel without caring about the feelings of the other person. Both the partners feel like what they are saying is less important and pushing their agendas.

Good: You talk rather than show emotion

When talking about important issues concerning the two of you, there is a chance that arguments will be raised when differences of opinions occur. However, this isn't the case with you. You both listen to each other's ideas and opinions in a calm and relaxed manner without getting triggered. This makes talking to your partner easier because there are less judgment and negativity involved.

Bad: You both lose temper during the conversation

If this is the case with you and no conversation reaches a fruitful conclusion, this means that the communication between you two needs to be improved. One or both of you are losing temper and being regressive in hearing what the other person has to say. These types of communications only add to the resentment partners feel towards each other, which also becomes a barrier to future conversations.

FIVE THERAPY EXERCISES FOR COUPLES TO IMPROVE COMMUNICATION

Coming to step three of the process of improving communication, this involves some fun and practical games and exercises that both the partners can play together to improve their conversations. You must keep in mind that these are just some general ideas to help start the conversation in the first place. After the initiation, it is solely up to you to how to take it from there. You can either go forward or return to step one of the problems.

Three by Three

To play this game, both the partners must write a list

of three things they like about their partners and three

things they dislike. Then, both spouses must exchange the notes and have a sensible discussion about both the good and bad. As a rule of thumb, the good must be appreciated so that the partner does more of it and the bad be noticed and avoided.

To make it more enriching, partners can also be more innovative with their contributions, such as listing three instances where their partner made them the happiest of the three times they expected more from them. Keep in mind that all the points exchanged must be discussed with an open mind with the end goal is improving communication. The more you know about your partner, the healthier your relationship will be. That way, you can attend to their needs and interests in a more supportive and appreciable manner.

Honesty Hour

Honesty hours is quite similar to the game above. However, rather than making a list of the things weekly, partners set aside an hour for healthy conversation every month or fortnightly.

Each partner gets an hour to express their feelings without judgment. The topic can be anything like talking about what things your partner lacks, what things you love about them, would like to improve about them or hate about them. During the hour, the listener must promise to listen and not hold any grudges or resentment. When the other person gets the chance, they should expect the same from their partner.

Once both the partners have expressed their concerns, problems, or failings, they can discuss them in greater detail and try to resolve issues that can be resolved.

Use the Five Languages of Love

We all have different ways of feeling loved. Some of us like to be appreciated verbally, whereas others care for more tangible things. Luckily, this game is ideal for any of those people as it allows couples to choose three from five different ways of expressing love.

Here's how you are going to play it.

You each get to write five different ways you want your partner to show you love. These could be anything like getting a back massage, talking about feelings, reading a book together, taking a bath, going on a long walk together, spending 30 minutes doing something your partner likes, presenting them with a thoughtful gift, praising them, etc.

Whichever options one partner chooses from the five options you offered them will tell you a great deal about them. For instance, if from the aforementioned things they chose getting a back massage, reading a book together, and going on a long walk together, this shows that they value physical connection more. On the other hand, if they chose praising them and talking about feelings, they crave an emotional connection and show of love.

When you understand your partner's need for long in the language they resonate with the most, it will become easier for you to plan things for them.

A FUN list

When playing this, each partner must write ten things on a piece of paper they would like to do with the other spouse. It can be the things they are interested in or things they want to try. The idea is to add some value to the time you two spend with each other and make the most of it. Not only will you know a lot about your partner, but it will also make the relationship more exciting. You each will get one day of the weekend to do one of the things from that list. Of course, you can opt for more than one but the goal should be to enjoy your time to the fullest.

Think of it as a bucket list with items you two want to do together. You can make one for every month or if you are too enthusiastic, make two! This way, you will always be looking forward to the end of the week and do something exciting together.

I feel...

As the name suggests, the "I feel..." game is another fun and heartening activity for couples to enjoy together. It allows couples to express themselves without being judged or critiqued. When we use "I" statements more often, we become better at the expression and formation of our thoughts. When we express it openly with our partners and they listen, it can improve the channel of communication.

During the week, make a list of all the things you thought

your partner did that hurt you. It could be raising their tone, not texting you back when coming late, saying no to go with you to a party you told them about weeks ago, and other such things. Write them down so that you can easily recall them when you two sit down to discuss them. Ask your partner to do the same so that they don't feel like an accused.

Take out some time every weekend and discuss all those pointers. Remember, there is only one rule of the game and that is not judging. Be courteous at listening to what the other person has to say without taking offend. Then try to discuss each situation and if they happened because of some other reason. For instance, the reason you forgot to text them back was that something extremely urgent came up and you had no time to look at your phone. The more they know the better.

What this will do is take away those feelings of hurt and help partners understand each other better.

CHAPTER - 5

BUILDING A DEEPER

CONNECTION

Now that we have discussed in detail how crucial communication is and what happens when enough of it isn't happening, the next step is to find out how we can deepen those communications and learn more about our partners and their respective needs.

Therefore, this chapter is solely dedicated to deepening the conversations with some meaningful topics that also help build intimacy between the couple. But before we do that, it is also important to discuss what conversations you two should start with to understand those primary needs. Later on, once we have passed the stage where we think we know them enough, we can work on improving or upgrading the level of intimacy between them.

THE 5 CONVERSATIONS YOU SHOULD BE HAVING WITH YOUR PARTNER

If you go asking people what the term "submissive" means to them, you will come across and an array of answers that can each start a debate. However, the most common definition that comes to mind, thanks to the 50 Shades of Grey, is that submissive is someone who allows someone to do things they want them to do. Wasn't it like that in the movie as well? Keeping Christian Grey aside from our thoughts for a minute, what if we dismiss this stigma associated with the word and think of it as something more positive and more compelling? Can we use willing in place of the term obedience – the one thing the submissive has to be?

Changing the definition to willing, can it help couples to develop stronger, meaningful and healthier relationships? One of the primary reasons partners avoid conflicts is because they are fearful of being wronged. This fear makes us lose our ability to agree, and we are in a defensive mode most of the time. What if we tell you that this fear is what is preventing you to achieve your happily ever after?

If we, for once, let communication flow, we might be able to see the beauty and magic of how it can transform our lives and drastically improve our relationships.

Here are some of the conversations you should have with your significant other.

I can't read your mind so what should I do?

A lot of partners say that they love their spouses but the next moment is fighting with them over things like what they ever did for them. To avoid conflicts and understand your partner more, you need to know their needs. Your partner needs to know that you aren't

Edward Cullen from Twilight that you would just read

their mind and know their needs. Alternatively, if you have certain expectations from them, tell them!

Most of the time, the reason we get upset with our partners is that we think that they should know what we want and we shouldn't have to remind them now and then. Moreover, we tend to generalize things and assume that our partners would get the hint. It doesn't work that way. If you want help with something, ask for it directly. For instance, imagine you told your partner that you had a busy day at work and you come home to a messy home with no meal prepared. You would get pissed because you expected them to do those things on their own. What they know is that you two do that together. You set yourself up for disappointment yourself.

Show me how to love you

If you know about the bestseller, The Five Love Languages, by Gary Chapman, you would understand that partners show and expect love in different forms. Some prefer deep conversations over sex. The idea is to use what works best for your partner and show them that you care for them. This works because many of us feel unloved or ignored in a relationship only because our partner fails to show us love in the way we understand or expect. Similarly, asking your partner how they would like to be loved allows helps you discover techniques that work for them the best.

Tell me how to touch you so that we can improve our intimacy

Partners are always motivated to meet each other's sexual needs. They both like dominance and want to prove that they are the best. How can they prove that? By giving you a memorable intimate time. When we get excited to give our partner a good time it shows them that their needs are cared for and acknowledged. It becomes a way of communicating with each other how much they are adored and admired. However, not everyone's definition of intimacy is the same and some think past the literal translation of it. This is exactly what you need to ask from your partner. Do they feel more touched and aroused when you do stuff other than sex with them? Do they have a specific need that gets them the high? For example, some partners love to role play. Your guy might be into some dirty talking or foreplay. They might even have sensitive areas they would like to be caressed. Ask them that so that both of you can have an even more enjoyable time together.

I want you to tell me how to make you feel better

A lot of times, we begin to assume things in the relationship, thinking we know our partners well. Though there is nothing wrong with knowing someone so personally, it can, at the time, be misleading as well. For example, you might think that the reason your partner is in such a bad mood is that you did something to piss them. But what if it isn't the case and they are upset about something else entirely? This assumption makes us a little defensive and we get agitated when their mood remains the same groggy. Sadly, we humans are afraid to show emotions. We keep them hidden from the world, specifically the vulnerable ones.

Jumping to conclusions on your own or expressing a similar emotion doesn't help anyone. Gratitude, empathy, and compassion, however, does. Ask them if there is something that you can do to make them feel better. Ask them how you can help to make the pain or anger go away. Ask them if they would rather talk about it or prefer having some space instead of all the assumptions and accusations?

Tell me what you want to do to me in bed?

One of the many reasons for infidelity in marriages is that partners are fearful of expressing what they want to do with their partners sexually. We all have some fantasies that we want to make happen. We think that talking about them too much with our partner may make us a pervert in their eyes and they might assume that they are not happy in the relationship. Some partners may also find things as disgusting or wrong if they have different beliefs. The fear of being judged, rejected, or criticized is what makes it even tougher.

If you think that your partner isn't as excited about sex as you are and rarely initiate, ask them how to make it better. Be open to converse about it and don't reject their ideas right away. Who knows the suggestions they have are, in fact, quite exciting and you end up liking them too?

WHAT CONVERSATIONS BUILD INTIMACY WITH PARTNER?

A lack of love and affection in any form makes the thing less valuable. Even if it is something as simple as baking a cake, if it isn't done wholeheartedly, the results won't be as joyous and comforting. Love is the essence of everything. There's a little dash of it into everything we do and marriage is no different. But like any other thing requires hard work, so does marriage. Intimacy is one aspect of any relationship that allows the partners to be connected to the highest levels. When they get intimate, their mind, body, and soul all connect on another level.

Building intimacy in a relationship is essential. It is what keeps the couple together. It creates moments of passion between them and keeps the attraction alive. It is also healthy as it releases dopamine and oxytocin from the brain which makes one feel loved and admired. However, many couples don't realize until late that what they have is just a casual physical connection. There are no feelings involved.

So how can you build/bring more intimacy into your relationship? You will be surprised that all you have to do is speak. Some conversations and actions help the partners stay close. From appreciating one another over the little things to asking them about their childhood, many conversations can bring the couple closer and improve their intimacy and connection. Confused?

Play Out Your Fantasies

The best way to build intimacy is to let each other know how and where to touch. Ask them what their fantasies are and try to play them out to get away from boring, casual intercourse. However, only ask them if you are willing to listen and act upon it. For example, if one partner likes dominance during the act or say, "like it rough," you should be willing to allow them to freely experience that with you. You both should be open to the other person's ideas without feeling ashamed or less valued. The more interested both partners are to play out their fantasies, the more they will look for chances to get intimate.

Keep in mind, this is just for improving physical intimacy. If the term intimacy is wider than what happens inside the room and encompasses elements like a deeper conversation, date nights, cuddling, or traveling together, then below are some tips to improve that.

Show Gratitude

One of the best ways to build intimacy with your partner is by expressing gratitude for all that they do for you. Even employees leave when they don't feel appreciated or recognized. You can't expect your partner to stay for long either. We all crave appreciation. Even if you don't have anything grand to be thankful for them, thank them for being there and helping you out with the work. Thank them for their presence, their supportive words, their ability to listen and much more. Make it a habit to show gratitude towards your partner so they feel more valued and accepted.

Be Supportive

As important is appreciation in any relationship, so is support. If your partner is going through something difficult, such as a health condition, grief, mental trauma, or emotional instability, it is your job as their partner to support them both emotionally and physically. You don't always have to use words, just sitting by their side and letting them know with your actions that you are there for them is appreciable. At times, we all feel weak, like we will just breakdown any minute. Having the knowledge that someone is there to hold us, and help us stand up in case we fall is reason enough to make you come closer to them. It is the same with friends.

If you don't know how to support them in their time of need, seek guidance. Ask them what they want you to do. Ask them how to make you feel better? Tell them that although you may not be able to magically remove all their pain, you are still trying to lessen it. This kind of reaffirmation goes a long way.

Talk About Life Experiences

Many people think that what is in the past should remain there, but it isn't true. If you have a past that keeps hurting you in some manner or keeps showing up in your face from time to time, let your partner know about it. Some people live with unresolved issues from their childhood they still haven't gotten over. These
issues can hinder the relationship with your spouse and

prevent it from becoming more intimate.

For instance, if your partner has witnessed physical abuse firsthand or hasn't gotten over the trauma of an earlier relationship, they may fear to be too intimate all together. How can a greater level of intimacy be achieved in this scenario? Expressing how you felt when that happened and how do you plan on moving past that is a conversation that you have with your present partner so that they can be helpful and supportive.

Converse About Self-Improvement

Talking about improving one's self in different areas of your life can also help you reconnect. For instance, if you know that your partner detests some habits of yours such as eating unhealthy or smoking or drinking too much, discussing how you would like to change them to be a better partner to them can also earn you some brownie points.

We all are flawed in one way or the other. Our partners live with some of the most annoying habits of yours without complaint but the same habits can sometimes become the reason for distance. Thus, talk with them about the things you would want to change about yourself so that you two can grow closer. Once you initiate, your partner will contribute too and try to give up things that annoy you.

Not everyone is comfortable being vulnerable in front of someone. It takes guts to allow someone to get a close look at who you are. Luckily, it is also the fastest way to build intimacy. Every partner craves to be the most important part of their partner's life. They want to know all about you, your dreams, aspirations, future goals, childhood traumas, and more. Opening up to each other enriches closeness. If you have someone brave enough to allow you to be a part of their dark and twisted life and also be there to support you in times when you feel vulnerable, you don't need anything more. If they still want you the way they did before you told them all about the things you feared sharing with anyone, then you already have the strongest connection with them.

Tell Them Why You Love Them

No one ever gets tired of hearing that someone loves them dearly. Those sweet words melt in our ears like butter in a heated pan. Keep telling your partner why you love them often and ask them the same. At first, you may feel like you are just fishing for compliments, but the biggest advantage will be improved intimacy. When partners express their feelings openly and don't shy away from saying that they love their spouse, it just makes everything seem sweeter.

However, note that you don't only have to tell them you love them, you have to focus on the "why." Why do you still feel attracted to them or can't keep your hands off them is what they need to know.

CHAPTER - 6

INTRODUCING NEW ROUTINES

Marriage may seem hard but that hard work is worth it. Putting in love, time and effort carefully into your matrimony is the recipe to a happy, strong, and everlasting partnership. The habits you two have and how you choose to express your love and emotions can have a significant impact on your marriage. It decides what kind of marriage you two will have. When we talk about habits, preferably the goods ones, we often refer to habits like saying "I love you" to your partner, supporting them in times of need, listening to them, paying attention, and giving them time, etc.

What we fail to realize is that there are also various other ways to keep the relationship strong.

In Part 6, we are going to be looking at what every-day routines convey the same message of "I love you" to your partner with even more love and compassion. We shall also look at how couples can convalesce their relationship with some fun activities at the end of the chapter to keep things interesting between you two.

DID I TELL YOU THAT I LOVE YOU?

Why some marriages are successful and some aren't depends on various factors. Sometimes, the partner no longer feels interested in each other or simply fall out of love. Other times, it can be the lack of communication on either of their parts where one partner usually feels left out and unacknowledged.

What helps in making any marriage successful are healthy habits that keep both the partners drawn towards each other all the time! Every marriage has challenges and arguments but how they are dealt with is the key to its success or failure. Imagine one partner has OCD and the other doesn't give a care in the world about the mess. Living together can be a nightmare for them with fights just waiting to start. If you look closely, their habits are what creates this crevice between them. However, if both of them can find themselves a middle ground, where the partner with OCD doesn't lose their mind coming home to a messy space and the other partner trying to clean up a little; this can turn into something less toxic and venomous.

So you see, it isn't always big gestures that make all the difference. It is the little things you do every day that keeps you two sailing smoothly, even on treacherous waters. The little things like bringing your partner breakfast in bed, ironing their clothes, preparing a meal, or simply just hugging and kissing them before leaving for work can make all the difference to them in the world.

98 These little things serve as reminders for your partner and they keep thinking about you all day and the

beautiful relationship you two have, says Lesli Doares, author of Blueprint for a Lasting Marriage, published in 2011, and also a marriage coach.

Everyday Habits and Routines that Say "I Love You"

Get Intimate

No other means of communication is as powerful and comforting as having sex. It releases the feel-good hormones in both of you and allows you to connect on a whole new level. However, when aiming for intimacy, don't just aim for the quantity. There is no point in having it three times a day if there is no excitement or thrill involved. Always aim for quality. How awesome it is is more important than how many times you do it. Also, it doesn't matter if it's a quickie in the shower or an hour full of lovemaking on a secluded island. Do it often and be in it wholeheartedly.

Have Going and Returning Rituals

Some couples never leave the house without kissing each other and some don't bother saying goodbye. Which one do you think is in for the long-run? Have a leaving and returning ritual where you two pause doing everything you were and greet your partner's goodbye or welcome home. These are the last few moments for you two to connect before you both leave for work. You gotta make it count!

Besides, it's harder to keep in touch all day, piled under brain-draining work and calls. When you prioritize the few minutes before one of you heads out for work every morning, it sets a positive tone and keeps your mood elated. No matter how tough the work gets, you still have that beautiful reminder to think about and know that something similar will be waiting when you return home.

Hug and Kiss

Well, that's a given but even science has proven how effective it can be. Kissing your partner each day for 30 seconds straight or hugging them for exactly 2 minutes releases oxytocin – a chemical also released during sex and usually when one is being touched with empathy and love. It creates an emotional bond, says Kim Blackham, a renowned family and marriage therapist. She believes that in today's ever hectic time, our kisses and hugs have become mechanical. We do them without even feeling a thing. Those little pecks and shoulder bumps have no meaning unless the other person actually feels something gushing through their body. Don't worry about the timing and try to dot every second. Just make your hugs and kisses extended.

Go for a Walk Together

Walking in the same direction makes couples feel like a team. The very act itself gets you out of the home and somewhere nice around the block. Going on a walk together also makes partners feel mentally sync as their destinations are the same. If you were to stand to confront each other, it gives the sense of a fight or conflict, as per Blackham.

Keep in Touch via Texts

In this world of calls and texting, you can and should always find some time to get in touch with your partner and let them know that they are being thought of. Nothing will bring a more genuine smile on their face than that. And now with the use of emoticons, you don't even have to type a lengthy message. Just a kiss emoticon can do the trick with an "I miss you" gif or a selfie. How hard can it be?

We all love these kinds of little anecdotes as they make us feel valued and loved. It also tells your partner that they are a priority in your life despite all the work that remains piled up.

Say Good Things to Each Other

Same as texts, compliments also go a long way to brighten up your partner's otherwise average day. Let them know that they look so good in that color or how great the tie goes with that shirt. Gentlemen, tell her that the shade of her lipstick makes you want to take them to bed, and every time they will reapply it during the day, they will think about you and be waiting for some hot sex under the sheets by the time you come home.

Appreciate Sweet Deeds

A lot of times partners selflessly do things for one another. They might wake up an hour early just so that they can make you breakfast before going to the office, fill your car with gas when they find it near the refill mark, get groceries as well as your favorite chocolate dip even though you forgot to mention it... These acts may be small but go a long way to show that there is someone who wants you to have the best things in life. Don't you think they deserve a little appreciation in return?

Whenever you notice your partner did something out of care for you without your asking, appreciate it. Not only will it reinforce that positive behavior but also show them that you notice and appreciate it. Couples who have been living together for long often overlook these little deeds which make the door feel resentful. Appreciate where required and let them feel a little pride and compassion.

Share a Meal

Even if you two have a day or night schedules, spare some time to have a nice and quiet meal at least once during the day. Eating in itself is an enjoyable thing and with a partner, it just gets better. If you have the time, get on your aprons and cook something together from scratch. Preparing meals together allows you to work as a team since the ultimate goal is the same. When we are motivated by the same goal, we tend to give our best and also have to do just half of the work. Win-win isn't it?

Sleep Together

Well, that seems obvious and exciting but some couples go to bed at different times. On the other hand, you may go to sleep the moment your head hits the pillow and

your partner might be a nocturnal animal who sleeps

later in the night. However, if you two can adjust your routines in a way that both of you sleep at the same time or at least get in bed together, it increases your chances of getting intimate, which is important as talked about earlier. Who knows, just a kiss can turn into some passionate kissing and then you two are taking off the clothes? See, that's an exciting thought, isn't it? Well, the only way to make it a possibility is for you two to be in bed simultaneously. If sex isn't the plan, you can always have some deep conversations before going to bed.

Reminisce About the Past

Talk about the time you two dating each other. Those are surely some memories you hold close to your heart. The love was new, the feelings were all so ecstatic and the urgency to meet each other was high. But the talk should only be limited to the good aspects of your relationship and not in a disagreeing manner. For instance, don't talk about how they used to bring you flowers every time you went out and they no longer do that. Instead talk about the times like how they planned a spontaneous road trip for you on your birthday and how much you still love them for it. Not only will that serve as an ego booster, but it will also give them the subtle hint that you want something similar to be planned again.

Leave the Tech Behind

Your alone time shouldn't be interrupted with the beeps and buzzes. When you two are together, give your tech a little break. Have a conversation, share the highlights of your day, and ask them about theirs. There is no point in sitting together when you are constantly disturbed by others. You both deserve each other's undivided attention and it can be very disrespectful if your partner feels that your phone is more important than them.

THREE FUN ACTIVITIES FOR COUPLES TO STAY STRONGER AS EVER

Who says a couple can't have some fun games nights together? Keeping up the spice in your relationship requires that you do things just for fun. And what better way to have fun than with some fun activities with your partner that will keep your #relationshipgoals worthy of a social media post.

Interested? Let's begin!

Five Things...Go!

This one is the simplest of all and requires nothing but just the two of you fully attentive towards each other. The only skill you actually need to have in order to play this game is your imagination. Here's how it is played.

Every time you plan to play this game, ask your partner to list any five things they are grateful for. There are countless questions you can ask and the partner has to come up with five things spontaneously. The only rule is that they can't think about them for too long. They have to answer fast.

The theme or the question can be changed each time depending on what you really want to ask them. For instance, you can even ask questions like name five superpowers you wished you had or what are the five things you miss the most about your childhood.

You can even ask them reasons as to why they feel so lazy doing the house chores. You get the point, right? The more creative your questions, the more creative their answers will be. The exercise can be extremely fun and engaging. The biggest advantage is that it will allow you two to loosen up after a tiring day at work, discover something new about yourself and have a laugh.

High and Low

This isn't a game but rather an exercise or practice that the couple should practice now and then. It promotes verbal communication between the couple and allows them to freely express themselves as well as listen to what their partner has to say to them.

This requires a peaceful and uninterrupted environment and preferably should be done in the latter part of the night when you both go to bed. Ask each other what were the best and worst things that happened that day. The best part will be their highest or high part of the day whereas the most disappointing would be regarded as the lowest or low part of their day.

The partner who is listening can rejoice about the best thing that happened to them that day and show empathy towards the thing that didn't go as planned. This is an excellent conversation starter as well as a great technique to tap into your partner's brain and take off some pressure as sharing always does that.

Fireside Chats

The term fireplace chat was coined during the time of President Franklin D. Roosevelt when he used an informal radio broadcast during his presidency to address the nation. People assumed that he did that while sitting calmly in a comfortable chair by the fireplace. The same theme applies to the couple who should imagine that they are sitting next to the president by a cozy fireplace addressing each other. The only difference will be the missing president and your spouse in their place.

The idea is to communicate as well as express your feelings in a decent, mature, and respectful manner without any cuss words or name-calling. Think of it as an argument but were both parties get a chance to place their cases in a relaxed manner and a calm environment. You can both decide on what to talk about and each partner should get 10 to 15 minutes to discuss how they feel about the subject.

To leave you with an example, you can both try to discuss a former fight that never concluded but calmly. The overall goal is to let out your feelings without feeling scared or ignored.

The pros of this game include getting a deeper insight into one another's behaviors as well as understand where they are coming from. It also helps partners to connect on a deeper level and discuss persisting issues amongst them without trying to kill each other.

CHAPTER - 7

EXPRESSING AFFECTION AND APPRECIATION

In any relationship, expression of feelings and emotions through verbal as well as non-verbal communication is a requisite. This is equally important for dating partners, newlyweds and couples who have been married for more than a decade. Expressing how we feel is always a good move because it tells our partners that they are treasured.

We all have different ways to show love. Some partners take it over the top and don't shy away with a public display of affection, whereas some are so secretive that one might start to think if they love us or not. In this chapter, we shall talk about the different ways our partners show love and also learn how we as their other half do our part with the appreciation as well.

AHH...THE THINGS I DO FOR LOVE

But before we do just that, here's the most important question, how do you know your partner loves you? Do they have a special way to tell you? Do they shout it off the balcony or do they whisper it in your ears every night? If they don't do any of that, they might use gestures instead. Still perplexed?

Here are some signs that say they love you irrespective of how many times they say or don't say it to you verbally. If you notice any of these, know that they do and that too, unconditionally.

How to Know Your Partner Loves You?

- They try new things with you. Even when they are as boring as visiting an art gallery and stare at a painting for hours when they are least interested or go watch a football game with you on their free day when they don't even know of which teams are playing.

- A partner who deeply cares for you and wants to learn more about your personality will try to take part in your extracurricular activities. Being involved in one hobby and doing things together, be it cooking courses or horse riding, tightens the bonds between the two of you and opens up your hidden qualities.

- They are protective of you. But not of the kind where they keep texting and calling you when you are a little late in returning home or feeling jealous of your friends. They just feel scared when you don't show up on time and worry for you. Also, they make sure to pick and drop you to and from home so that you don't have to worry about tagging with others or taking a cab.

- They are affectionate. They don't just reserve their emotions for when you two get intimate. They understand that physical intimacy isn't the only thing you two have. They are also up for spooning, cuddling, and looking at each other in the eyes for as long as required. When in public, they don't feel embarrassed to be seen with you. They are the first ones to hold hands or keep touching you one way or the other just to let you know they are there.

- They are always respectful. Not only generally, but they also respect your views about different things, value your advice and decisions, are careful with the language they use around you or the kids. All these are signs that they love you dearly.

- They act gentlemanly. Even if it has been more than a decade since you two tied the knot, they still treat you like the king/queen. They open the car door for you, pull out your chair, get the kids to school on days you feel tired, make you breakfast in bed, unload the groceries for you and more...

- They love you for who you are. They don't try to change things about you. They just accept the way you are. Even on your worst day, they aren't the ones to walk out the door. They also make you feel good about yourself. They never shy away from giving you the validation that you are the best version of yourself.

- They are willing to fight for you. It is also a sign of their undying love that they make sure you always have their back. You feel safe when you are with them. You know that if things go wrong, they will be there for you, ready to defend or fight for you. If required, they will be willing to put their life at risk just to ensure you feel safe.

- They say they are proud of you. Even when your accomplishments aren't big or significant, they still tell you that they are proud of you. They keep reminding you that you have come a long way and improved both as a person and a partner. Basically, whatever you do seems amazing to them.

How to Express Your Love More Powerfully

Some people do just fine without praises and reminders of love. They are rarely the first ones to initiate lovey-dovey conversations, they don't send mid-day texts about missing you, or greet you with a hug and kiss on the door when you come home. And then, some can never have enough of it. They constantly need to be reassured that their partner loves them. They expect big gestures, surprises, and thrill of the relationship.

Whichever is the case with you, we say you say it. In fact, shout it out if you must. No one deserves to feel not loved by their significant other. Remind them from time to time and not just with your words but also with your actions. Below are some great ways to express your feelings using both verbal and non-verbal gestures to strengthen the bond with your beloved!

- Do nice things for them – This can be anything grand or small like taking their car to the auto repair or doing the laundry. Even the smallest of gestures go a long way and your partner will surely notice.

- Give each other time – As a couple, your partner should be your most important priority. Make sure that they know that! Set aside some time every day to just sit with them and have a chat, even for a few minutes over dinner or a drink. Let them know that you love having them around and value their company.

- Compliment them – "Hey, you look nice with your hair down" or "You look so handsome in that sweatshirt" are examples of compliments that you can give to boost each other's self-confidence and morale.

- Help around the house – Even if doing the dishes is your partner's job, do it for them when they look tired or "not in the mood." Sometimes, household chores can seem like a burden on one partner. Offer help and try to help your spouse in domestic chores. There's nothing unmanly about it.

- Plan a spontaneous date night – Unplanned dates are the best. One minute you are sitting home and the next minute you get a text from your partner telling you to get ready as they will pick you up from work and take you to that new fancy place that just opened up. Even if it isn't a fancy place, a night away from the cooking and the dishes is a treat itself.

- Perhaps a movie night – Hey, who says you have to go out for a movie? You can always enjoy one in the comfort of your homes. To upstage love and affection, ask them to pick one out!

- Do things they like – Let them plan an outing or an activity that they would like to do. Trying new things with your partner is always fun. The best part: you might like the change from doing the same things over and over again.

- Go tech-free – When together, try to minimize the use of technology. It can be extremely annoying and disrespectful when you pay more attention to your phone than them during your time together.

- Kiss them – Make it a habit to bid them by and greet them on their way back home with a kiss. It just sets the mood right. Coming home to a loving spouse just brightens up the day and the deeper and passionate the kiss, the better.

- Text inappropriate – Who said texting is just for the kids. Be playful and keep your partners interested in some enticing and sexy texting during the day. This will give them a hint of what they can expect from you when they come home and believe us, they will be there before their usual time!

- Buy them something nice – If they have been talking about a new game or gadget, if you have the means, buy it for them and surprise them. When they ask you why you bought it for them, tell them that you just felt like it.

- Anticipate their needs – Be proactive. If they like their clothes pressed and hung before they come out of the bath, make sure that it is done. Go out of your way to fulfill their needs and make sure they don't have to ask for it.

- Listen carefully – Carefully listen to every word that

comes out of their mouths. You don't want to miss out on any details that may hold importance. How to be an effective listener? Go back to Part 1 and look at the tips at the end of the chapter.

- Look each other in the eyes – Eye contact lets the other person know that you are attentively listening to whatever it is you are saying. The more attentive they think you are, the more validated and heard they will feel. Even that is a great way to express your love.

- Hug it out – Whenever you hug, make sure that it isn't just your bodies colliding into one another, your hearts should too! Aim for that and extend the hug for as long as you can. It will do wonders for your relationship.

- Be their cheerleader – Support them in their journeys like their biggest fan or loyalist companion. They should know they have the best people on their team cheering them on.

- Show acceptance – We often assume that love is all about giving and giving. But it is also about accepting what the other person has to give. They may not bring you flowers every night like your friend's husband but do something equally special. Don't disregard their show of affection and passionately accept what they are offering you.

- Leave cute notes for them – Who doesn't like surprises, especially when they come in the form of cute little handwritten notes you find in the pocket of your shirt or your lunchbox at the office? We all do and so will your partner. GUARANTEED!

I CAN'T THANK YOU ENOUGH FOR THE THINGS YOU DO!

Appreciating someone involves giving someone credit for what they did. It also means giving them value and when we use appreciation in terms of a relationship, giving one value is important. It tells the person being appreciated what they mean to you and where they stand. When we avoid appreciation in a relationship or fail to consider it crucial, we change the dynamics of it. How partners will respond to each other's needs, how they will give each other time, how they will work as a team to take joint decisions etc. All of these change. When one of you feels devalued in a relationship, they eventually lose interest in the whole idea of staying together and that is why arguments start to brew up.

The Importance of Appreciation in Relationships

It is important to note that it isn't only partners who value appreciation, all humans do. Not appreciating someone for the things they do doesn't sit well with anyone. In relationships, when one of the spouses feel less valued or treasured. They may think that they are being taken for granted. When one begins to think in that manner, the next stage involves feeling resentment, frustration, and avoidance. We begin to think if working this hard trying to save it is worth it or not.

Let's picture a scenario, shall we?

Imagine, you drop the kids to school every day. To do that, you get up earlier than your partner, make your kids breakfast, get them dressed, out of the door, and into the car. Then you drop them at the gate before the final bell rings, and this has continued for several years. On the way home, you get stuck in traffic and reach home 10 minutes later than usual. Your partner opens the door and starts yelling at you for not waking them up earlier. They blame you for getting you late from work and call you lazy.

First off, you never appreciated the fact that they do all of that every day no matter how tired they were last night. Secondly, you just ruined their day with all the yelling and called them incompetent and lazy. Imagine you had to be the one to drop the kids to school, get them ready, and serve them breakfast? Would you have liked the attitude of your partner?

Would you not have pondered if the relationship is worth it after all? Probably not.

What seems so simple just because you always find it done doesn't mean the work is any less than what you do. If you had to do it, you would have felt bone-tired before you even reached the office. So gentlemen, thank your wives for putting food on the table, cleaning up the house, doing your laundry, and looking after the kids all by themselves, and ladies be thankful for a husband who helps you with the chores, gets you groceries on the way back home, and takes you out for date nights.

As a couple, you both have to do your part of thanking

and appreciating each other. You might find it stupid to thank your wife for doing the dishes or your husband for taking out the trash, but do it. Failing to appreciate them for such menial work means that you think of your work as bigger and more important than theirs and it can be very demeaning. This is the point where the balance in the relationship starts to shake or go off-scale.

There are other reasons to appreciate your partner as well. For instance:

- It just makes them happy. They feel they have accomplished something big and also that you notice all that they do for you.

- It makes it easier for them to appreciate you too. Sometimes, all someone needs is a little encouragement or initiation and they learn to reciprocate.

- It shows that you are actually glad to have them in your life and tells them that you are sincerely happy for their presence and all that they do.

- It also shows that you truly respect them which only amplifies your respect in their eyes. You see acknowledgment works both ways. To acknowledge and appreciate someone's work, you must be attentive and considerate.

- It makes them feel special, treasured, and honored.

LEARNING TO APPRECIATE – IT'S NOT THAT HARD!

Showing gratitude is a lot like expressing love. Some of the acts such as spending time with them and showering them with gifts, compliments, and surprises also show appreciation as well as love. Showing gratitude nurtures your relationship with your partner. It creates a healthy environment for both to work as a team and in unison to accomplish future goals together. When we appreciate someone for something that they did, we are subtly telling them that they did well and it makes them feel proud.

In this section, how about we learn how to show gratitude to your partner for all the good that they do every day?

First off, when expressing your love, be creative. Don't just say a bland "thank you." Although that would still work, how about getting a little creative with how you show gratitude? How about using different phrases or leaving little notes and reminders on their phones? Saying thank you all the time will ultimately lose its charm. Therefore, use phrases like:

- I am so grateful that you...

- I can't thank you enough for...

- Oh, lucky me for having you as my partner...

- What did I ever do to deserve someone as good as you...

- No one does it better than you...

Appreciate Their Intention for Helping You Out

Sometimes partners go out of their way to show that they care. They will take out the trash, soothe the crying baby, help the kids with their bath, do the dishes, get groceries, or help with making dinner without asking. Don't take that for granted or they will think there is no point in doing them. I appreciate the fact that they cared enough to think of them doing them without asking. Also, acknowledge that they didn't do it just for the praise but because they care about you.

Thank Them by Giving Them a Break

As we grow older, the one thing we want the most is peace and quietness. We wish that everything will fall in its place itself and that we won't have to work. If your spouse wishes for the same, give them a few hours of complete quietness to themselves. Take the kids out of the house and let them be... Ask them to take a break from all their duties for the day and do whatever they want to. If they want to go to the park, a carnival or the market, tell them that it is completely up to them and that they won't be interrupted.

Appreciate the Thoughtfulness

If your spouse took up some chores but failed to do it like you would have done, then don't judge them on the results. Judge them on the thoughtfulness and the efforts. Similarly, if they left a crease on your shirt, burned the dinner a little or forgot to get you something from the list of groceries, don't make them think that all their time and effort were wasted. Be thoughtful and get over it. It is the thought that matters and not the result.

Prepare Them a Special Meal or Take Them Out On a Date

If your partner loves something that you cook but you rarely cook it because it takes so much time and effort, make it a habit to cook it more often as a token of appreciation for them. Don't worry about the mess but focus on how happy they will feel. If they like something that their mother made for them when they were a kid, get the recipe and make it exactly like that. You won't believe the amazement and joy that would show on their faces. To add some more feel to it, light a few candles, dim the lights, play some soft music, and dress nice.

If cooking isn't your best suit, how about taking them out to a place of their liking? Perhaps, a place that makes them nostalgic or serves a special that they love. Or better yet, take them to the place you both went for a date to relive the good ol' times.

Thank Them for Being with You Through Tough Times

We often take our partners for granted when counting our blessings and success. We fail to concede how crucial a part they planned without asking in helping you achieve all those things. Your partner was there beside you when you were up all night working on a project, your partner was also there to look after you during your illness, your partner was the one who did all the household chores without asking, your partner was the one who stood beside you and supported you when you thought you had failed. They were always there, being your biggest fan and motivating you to keep aiming for the skies. Don't you think they deserve some appreciation for all that?

Be sure to tell them that today!

Praise Them Openly

The praises and thank-yous shouldn't just be for inside the bedroom, let the whole world know how grateful you are to have them in your life. Partners, especially women, love it when their husbands gloat about how helpful and wise they are. Let your extended family know how much of a help they are and how compromising and understanding your partner is. That will surely have them on cloud nine and make their day.

Say Thank You with A Personalized Gift

It can be anything from a gift card to their favorite clothing brand, a bouquet of their favorite flowers, a spontaneous trip, tickets to their favorite game, a spa coupon, a customized stationery item they can use in their office, a signed t-shirt of their favorite band, a DVD of their favorite game, or a special sweet delivery of a box of chocolates they never saw coming. When buying them a gift, think about what they would like the best. Make it as personalized as possible so that when they receive it, they know just how much work must have gotten into it.

CHAPTER - 8

IDENTIFYING WHAT ISN'T RIGHT

Sometimes, in a relationship, we can't seem to disregard the thought that something isn't right. We don't know how to exactly point out the change but just know. Our gut tells us so. We sense a change in our partner's behavior. They seem distant, disinterested, or just unconcerned about things anymore. First, we think that perhaps the work has gotten to them and that is why they are not interested in anything concerning you but as more time passes, you realize that it isn't about showing less interest in you. They aren't as devoted to your kids or family either. They forget important dates, come back later than usual, say that they have eaten with friends, and go to sleep right away. They rarely compliment how you look and fail to notice any changes you made to your appearance, hair, or dress when they used to.

The more this continues, the more boggled your mind becomes. A hundred different things are going on in your head. Could they be cheating on me? Have they found someone else? Do they not find me attractive anymore? Have they fallen out of love? Before you go mad with all

121

the circulating thoughts in your mind, look if they are depicting any of the signs stated below to confirm your doubts at first and then have a conversation about it with them in detail. Unless you are sure you can't doubt them saying, you just felt something was off. They might feel offended or hurt knowing your views about them. Thus, always be sure before accusing someone of infidelity

IS MY PARTNER NO LONGER INTERESTED IN ME?

They Are Always Busy

At the end of the day, it is all about priorities, and as their spouse, you should be their first, no exceptions! If they have started treating you like a second option or taking you for granted, it is a sign they have lost interest in you.

They Don't Talk Much

If communication has become non-existent between the two of you, it means they couldn't care less about your feelings, emotions, or thoughts. If they cared, they would have always figured out something to talk about.

They Keep Blaming You

Constantly blaming you or torturing you with name-calling is a sign that they are deliberating trying to distance you from themselves. A classic sign of disinterest!

They Keep Pointing Out Your Flaws

122 If they were always praising you for little things a while ago and have now become downright nasty and

determined at pointing out your flaws to you, it means they no longer find you or your personality interesting.

They Have Changed You

But sadly, for the worst. You no longer smile like you used to, feel agitated most of the time, are confused, and lost in your thoughts.

They Don't Include You in Anything

They make decisions without you, are not bothered about sharing their plans, will disregard any of the plans you make and so on. They are trying to subtly tell you that they no longer want to have anything to do with you.

They Don't Apologize Anymore

They would always leave a text about being late and try to make it up to you when they returned home but no such thing happens now.

They Have Excuses for Everything

Apart from empty apologies, they also make excuses for everything. They won't come with you to the party or at a family gathering, they won't complete their part of the chores, and they will say they are tired when you try to initiate sex... another one of their excuses!

They No Longer Care About Your Welfare

They are less empathetic or rarely show any concern over your mood, your state of mind or your physical 123 exhaustion.

They Forget Things

Be it birthdays, a plan made a week ago, or an invitation to a wedding you have stopped bragging about all week. They tend to forget or overlook the things that matter the most to you which also shows that their ability to listen attentively has also decreased.

They Treat Others Better

They will have the humblest of smiles for their friends and even show interest in what a stranger has to say to them, say a man at the grocery store, but act groggy and frustrated with you all the time.

They Have or Are Cheating On You

Cheating is a sure-tell sign that confirms their disinterest. They have fallen in love with someone else or are having an affair, which is why you no longer appeal to them as a prospective candidate for a partner.

14 SIGNS MY PARTNER HAS COMMITTED INFIDELITY

As stated earlier, if it isn't just a lack of interest, it could be infidelity. Sadly, it is one of those problems in marriages that take a toll on the partner cheated on. It is the biggest obstacle to move past and often considered an immediate deal-breaker. A lot of times, we are so blinded by the love for our partners that we fail to notice the signs of adultery. It is usually someone else who throws the idea our way and then that becomes the only thing on our minds. We instantly begin to recognize the changes in their behavior, in their tone, in their appearance and all.

However, one can't just confront someone on a few hunches they have. Since it is something that you can't go back from, make sure that if you are accusing someone of having an affair, you have solid proof to show. Because the chances of the other partner accepting their fault are close to nil, you better have everything together.

Look at the classic signs that cheating partners often depict without realizing and thus are caught cheating.

They Are Unreliable

There was a time when you were the center of all their attention, but now you feel like you are no more than an afterthought in their lives. This can mean that they are unfaithful with you.

He/She Kisses Less Often

If they have started to avoid initiating a kiss and austerely avoid it during sex unless you pull them right into it, then they are cheating. They may also bail on the foreplay, avoid making eye contact, and time out their sex, it is a sign that their mind and heart are wandering someplace else.

He/She Is Always "Working"

Is he usually late? Does he/she always say that they are at the office and working on something important? It could be their new object of affection... just saying. When a partner cheats, they will try their best to minimize their contact with their spouses and use excuses to stay out of the house. They just feel a little guilty when they are with you, but boy does that stop them from cheating? Certainly not!

Every Time You Confront Him/Her, They Call You Crazy

Even if in just some casual banter, you bring up the topic of cheating, they start to act all weird and call you crazy for even thinking like that. No one likes to be caught red-handed and a cheater will always say they haven't cheated. So take the hint if they act too surprised on the idea that you called them a cheater.

His/Her Dressing Style Changes

If he had a difficult time suiting/dolling up for any occasion previously and has started to do it too often now, it is again a sign that they are trying to impress someone. Also, if they seem obsessed with going to the gym or shopping for more sharp-looking/sexy clothes, it could mean they are cheating.

He/She Gets Angry When Questioned

Where you were until now just riles him/her up like the Hulk. He/she hates being questioned about their whereabouts. Their stories won't match, their tone and pitch will change paces and they will try to avoid talking about it altogether.

He/She Stays Up Late

A sudden shift in their bedtime routine indicates an

affair. Cheating partners consider a partner's sleeping time as the safest to text or message their new love interest.

His/Her Stories Seem Inconsistent

Sometimes they won't say a word about where they were and sometimes they would give away too much. When asked if a friend was there with them too, they will not only confirm their presence but also tell you about all the other people who were there, including someone's pets. Too much information is another sign that there is something fishy going on or else they won't be this particular about it.

There Is No Intimacy

Not just physically, but you also find them emotionally distant from you. Even when they are with you, their mind doesn't seem to be. They have also lost interest in sex and always make excuses like being tired, not in the mood, had chili beef in the office and feeling bloated, etc.

They Never Put Their Phone Down

If they seem to be stuck with their phone all the time and even taking it with them when taking the trash or going for a bath, it is a sure tell sign that there is something in that phone they don't want you to know about.

He/She Pays Attention to Himself/Herself

It's always appraisable that your spouse dresses up for you, but if they are suddenly worried about how they look naked or whether they should get a bikini wax or not, it's probably an effort to look good for someone other than you.

You Only Get One-Word Answers from Them

You sense a barrier in your communications because they have resorted to a yes, no, or hmm at most. When partners lose interest in their spouses or are having an affair, they fear to communicate too much. They want to play it carefully and not say or do something that would get them caught.

They Are Spending Too Much

If all of a sudden you notice too many credit card bills and receipts in their pockets and yet you don't receive any supposed gifts, then someone else is on the receiving end of them. When asked, they will always have an explanation over how they had to lend some money to a friend, how they had to pitch in the last minute for an office party for a guy's farewell or how they had to pay a medical bill of some relative.

He/He's Doing Things They Hated Before

Remember the time you asked them to go golfing with you and they flat out refused and joked about how it's an old man's sport? Look who is all polo shirts and hats now! If their interests have changed all of a sudden and they are doing stuff they hated, know something is up.

CAN WE GO BACK TO HOW WE WERE?

So my partner committed infidelity. What now?

Despite how people put it, infidelity doesn't have to mean the end of the relationship.

But your partner hurt you where you never thought they would hurt you. They broke the solemn vow of your marriage, they shattered your confidence and self-esteem and broke the house you built so lovingly for them. Are you willing to see past all that and accept them for who they are? Can you rebuild your house again? Can you find love for them in your heart again? Can you live with the fact that they cheated on you for the rest of your life? Can you promise to trust them again?

Besides, there isn't just one partner to blame for the affair. A lot of times, the reason men cheat on their wives is that they don't feel valued or appreciated. Although this doesn't give them any right to cheat, the other partner also needs to understand whether they had been to fault or not. In Part 3, we learned how a lack of communication or interest in your partner's needs and feelings can create a rift in between, could it be the reason why they sought the same from someone else? Or perhaps, you always had an excuse for not having sex with them which led them to other places to fulfill their physical needs? It could have just been physical, you see?

If you still love them and they have truly repented about their behavior, it is still going to be very difficult to forgive them. They hurt you immensely, they broke your trust, they took you for granted, and they chose someone over you. These are all thoughts that will keep your mind occupied for some time. However, if after living separated, you both realize that you two are miserable without each other and think about seeing someone, you must know that it is you who has to start the journey, not them. Their job, today and forever, will now stay committed to you and prove to you that you are above everyone.

Your job, however, is to forgive them – the hardest thing in the world.

Regardless of that, if you have decided to stay as a couple and see past this, know that forgiveness can be extremely powerful. In some cases, it helps the couple develop an even more meaningful relationship than before.

The Power of Forgiveness

Firstly, you must understand that forgiveness isn't about the other person. It is about you gifting yourself the ability to see past someone's wrongdoing and still accept them. It isn't about letting them but rather yourself off the hook. In marriage, forgiving your partner for cheating on you is considered strength as it allows the cheating partner to see the good in you and how much of a bigger person you are. It doesn't make you come out as weak but rather stronger than ever. It is the first step towards healing the relationship and learning to trust them again. Forgiveness is also about giving yourself, your kids, and your partner the future you wanted for them, free of anger and hurt.

Restoring Trust in the Relationship

If you have been cheated on by a partner, you must understand the earth-shattering effect it can have on the trust in your relationship. The good thing, however, is that trust can be rebuilt. Of course, it will take time to fully trust your partner again after what they did, but it is a possibility. Both of you will have to work as a team to restore the balance in the relationship so that, one day, you both can go back to how you two were when you fell in love.

You must also understand that the process of healing will take time. The cheating partner mustn't expect things to go right between you two overnight or think that one apology is enough to resettle terms in the marriage.

Below are some tips to help you two restore the lost faith in the relationship and rebuild the trust.

Be Honest

If you have been wronged, you have every right to be angry with your partner and express that anger. Trying to keep things inside will only suffocate you more. You need to let your partner know how hurt you are and how you expect to be repaired. A lack of communication can only make matters worse where the other partner will think you haven't forgiven them yet. Let them know everything honesty like how much time do you need, if you feel comfortable with them in the same room or not, or how you plan to work this out. The more open you are about your emotions and feelings, the better for you. Besides, it is always a good idea to vent things out so that your mind takes a break from all that thinking.

Let Them Witness Your Pain

Sometimes, the partner that has wronged their spouse is so paralyzed with guilt that they keep asking for forgiveness over and over again. They must understand that what you are going through is painful and is a result of what they have done. Now they must bear witness to it and allow you time to grieve completely. They should know not to keep insisting on forgiving you or trying too hard to make things right.

Don't Expect Cheap Forgiveness

Asking for forgiveness over and over again can also add to the frustration the cheated partner feels and just to get the cheating partner out of their hair, they might vent out their anger saying that they have forgiven them when, in reality, it isn't the case. This stops the process of grief midway and one never fully comes out of it. On the other hand, the cheating partner might take is a weakness and use it against you for any future infidelities. Therefore, be patient with your words and don't act with anger. If there is nothing nice you can offer in terms of words, remain silent and let your partner know that you need more time.

Share the Blame

As we discussed earlier, how both partners can be at fault. Although the cheating partner should take 100%

of the blame as they could have always talked it out with you and let you know of your intentions beforehand, you should also take responsibility for keeping them in an unhappy or ungrateful union. If the infidelity happened because the partner felt less heard or unappreciated, then the wronged partner must accept it and know that some part of the hurt and isolation that they have brought upon themselves is because of the way they treated their spouse.

This knowledge and acceptance can help the process of healing and allow them to be more emotionally available for their partner the next time around.

Set Some Ground Rules

Before forgiving the adulterous spouse, the wronged partner must lay down some ground rules for how things will be between them from now on. It doesn't have to be a revenge list since the goal is to get back together. Point out how they can earn back the lost trust and respect in your eyes. Some other rules can be keeping no secrets between them from now on, making more time for the family, removing passwords from their phone and laptop, allowing the other person to see what they are doing without hiding or closing the tabs, etc. If they comply to all of these, it means they really are up for going at the relationship again. It also gives you some power over them and makes them feel like dictated and dominated, which is great at the end of the day because let's face it, they brought it upon themselves.

Redefine Physical Intimacy

In the beginning, there might be days where you feel yuck while being kissed or hugged because the voices in your head keep shouting cheater, cheater, cheater!

The biggest challenge between partners starting over after a cheating episode is healing between the sheets. How to allow them to be physical with you when you don't know if they are truly thinking about you or just faking it? Besides, you may feel less confident about your body and avoid getting close to them. It is fathomable and a very normal reaction to have.

On the other hand, when you do allow them the chance to be physical with you, both of you have completely different thoughts going on in your mind. They might try to please you in bed, which can result in them tiring out or performing poorly. You, on the other hand, might interpret it as a lack of interest. So basically, you two will be back at square one.

The best way is to communicate how each of the partners feels and shares their fears. This can help foster sexual intimacy, and the vulnerability both feel can cause a spark in the relationship again.

Ignore the Sayings

Once a cheater, always a cheater, as many put it. However, this is rarely the case. Partners who are drowning in guilt and shame spend their whole life trying to make up for that one mistake they made, even after their partners have long forgiven them. Thus, ignore the labels and trust your instincts instead. If you think that your partner is guilty and ashamed about it, then give them another chance to prove it. If they really want to get back with you, they will do everything in their power to win your heart again.

And if there is anything you do wish to remember, remember this: some people learn their lesson the first time!

Let Go

The last and most important point is to let go. This may seem difficult at first, but you need to delete the mental image of them busy with someone else. You have to stop thinking about how many times it happened or how your partner felt in those moments. The clearer your head, the more open it will be to the idea of getting back together. You need to free your mind and soul from all such thoughts because, at the end of the day, they are only hurting you and your mental peace.

Know that the power to let go is indeed precious. Not everyone has it in them to move past something like this and if you have decided to, then you are no less than a warrior yourself. Embrace this newfound ability within you and start working on building your relationship from scratch again.

CHAPTER - 9

HOW TO IMPROVE YOUR SOCIAL SKILLS

As we said, humans are social beings. Each individual feels the need to be loved and accepted in society. Social interaction plays a significant role in our lives.

While researchers have proven that extroverts are generally more successful in their endeavors and more social, it's not a bad thing to be an introvert.

Introverts are great observers and listeners. They will absorb everything around them, although they might not contribute to a conversation, even if they have something beneficial to offer. They are shy and often insecure. Fear of saying the wrong thing and coming off as foolish will keep an introvert from opening up in conversation. This can be an obstacle in the path to success for the introvert.

When a person is able to present his ideas accurately and connect with others, there are more chances of being successful and it becomes easier to achieve success.

ESSENTIAL SOCIAL SKILLS

Today, people spend their time mostly in the digital world instead of the real world. You have probably seen those types of people–they sit across from each other at a restaurant table and they are on their phones, never looking up, never conversing.

When it comes time to converse, they have limited words for the other as they are too wrapped up in whatever it is that's on their phone distracting them.

We see this more often with the younger generation, but the older generation is not immune from this antisocial behavior.

The digital age has changed the way we communicate, and it's not always for the better. Sure, it saves time when we can message a coworker instead of walking to their office. It saves time to be able to text the boss when they're out of town rather than to leave a message at the hotel where they are staying or having them paged when they're at a conference. Those were the good ole days before the advent of the cell phone. Often, emergencies had to wait, and employees were left unsure of what to do until the boss returned.

Sadly, the advent of cell phones led to the fracture of our social skills. This is why we sometimes need to relearn these skills to bring up back up to par. What we gained in social skills in our youth can fall into the abyss with technology.

138 Here is a list of skills that can help to increase your skills

and be successful in the social sphere.

Disagree in an agreeable manner

The underlying basis of good communication is proper understanding. If someone says something that is not in line with your thinking, you need to be diplomatic about disagreeing.

You can begin by saying, "In all due respect..." This tells the person that you respect their opinion, but you are of a varying one. Then you can give your point of view. By letting the person you're speaking with know that you understand their opinion, you won't come off as confrontational or as a know-it-all.

You can also begin with a phrase such as, "I see your point, but..." A non-confrontational and non-disagreeable segue will put you on level ground.

Do not assume things

Assumptions can be dangerous. Never assume something. Always be sure before speaking. We have all heard of or been in situations when someone assumes something, and it's the wrong assumption. Conjecture can cause hurt feelings and much more. Assumptions aren't more than mere gossip, and gossip won't improve anyone's social status, and it's certainly not something you want to include in your skillset.

Smile

A smile can work wonders. It is easy to make friends 139 and break the barriers between people by offering a pleasant smile. It can make others feel happy and show them that you care for them.

Maintain eye contact while talking

When you are talking to someone, your eyes should be on them. This doesn't mean to stare at them. It's okay to look away from time to time; however, eye contact lets the other person know that you are genuinely interested in what they're saying. When you don't look at the speaker, they will assume you're distracted. You might be listening intently, but they will assume otherwise. This is why assumptions aren't a good thing.

This also brings us back to our conversation about the digital age. When someone is speaking to you, don't be looking at you phone, or worse, texting. You need to focus on the speaker, not on Facebook or texting your significant other. Not only is it rude, but it tells the other person that you're not interested in what they're saying.

Be upbeat

Keeping a conversation positive and upbeat will relax the person you're talking with, and the more relaxed, the more comfortable the conversation.

Surely, there's been a time when you've had a tense conversation, or there was an awkwardness that crept into it. When you remain upbeat, you can keep any awkwardness away.

Be cognizant of your body language

When you are speaking one-on-one or in a group, you want to be relaxed and hold yourself in a non-threatening way. By that, it means you don't want to appear disinterested or as if you're ready to dart at the first open opportunity.

Keep your hands away from your face, watch how you stand or sit, and be cognizant of the position of your legs and arms. Don't tilt your head so far to one side that you appear to be disinterested or bored.

Get involved

The best way to build healthy relationships is to be involved in extracurricular activities. This is especially good for those who are trying to develop better social skills but are shy or don't have many contacts. Getting involved in a hobby or sport, take classes, attend church functions, etc. There's an endless list of ways to meet others and to build on social relations.

Offer praise

You should make it a point to praise others. Always look for opportunities to appreciate the good work done by others. It helps to create an amicable environment, and everyone feels happy when their hard work and efforts are given due recognition.

You don't want to do it to patronize someone because that can be very transparent. You need to be sincere and don't ramble on as if you're trying to convince the person that you are sincere. A simple "Great work" or "You really knocked that one out of the ballpark" lets that person know you are genuine and appreciate their work.

You can offer compliments as well, again, as long as you're sincere. Don't tell a female coworker that you love her scarf if it's completely tacky with the rest of her outfit. Don't tell a male boss that his tie is awesome if it looks like it was stolen from a clown.

Praise and compliments go hand-in-hand with honesty. A pretentious compliment will not go unnoticed.

Have good intentions

Always have good intentions. No matter what the situation, make sure your intentions are well-placed. Everyone makes mistakes; however, as long as it's not done with ill intentions, others will realize it.

Be helpful

Strive to help others, even when you might not be in the mood. Of course, you don't want to force help. If someone doesn't want it, you simply tell them that you're available if they change their mind. At least you made the offer.

Take care of your health

Everyone likes energetic people. A person's energy level depends on their health. The better you feel, the more confidence you'll have. You want to maintain a healthy diet and sleep habits. We won't elaborate on this as there's many books on the market that will guide you to better health if that's what you need.

Attitude counts

Have you ever spent a day with Debbie or Donnie Downer? It's certainly no fun to be around someone who always sees the glass as half-full, or worse, empty. They have a tendency to bring down others with their negative attitude.

You definitely don't want to be that person. You want to have a positive attitude, especially around your coworkers. A negative attitude can cost you a promotion. When looking at employees to advance, an employer will look for the employee with the most positivity. Those with a positive attitude are more successful and get father ahead in life.

You want to live your life so that when you leave this earth, people are sad and not celebrating that you're gone and took your miserable attitude with you. It's a sad fact. No one wants to be remembered for being cranky and uncooperative.

Be your best

Be what you are because that is the reason why people are fond of you. There is no need to pretend. You should display your best traits and be positive, flexible, and happy. People will love to associate with you and enjoy your friendship.

The same thing is applicable to the place where you work. There is no need to alter your personality to keep up with the company culture. You just have to be mindful of certain things and adjust to various social situations.

EFFECTIVE COMMUNICATION SKILLS FOR THE WORKPLACE

Communication is the center of any business. To be effective, everyone needs to have excellent communication skills from the CEO to the custodian.

Even if you are highly qualified and also know how to do your work very well, if you lack social skills it may be tough for you to fit in with your coworkers.

If you have a job that requires you to interact with your colleagues and clients every day, it is important to learn and brush up the social skills that are required. You may be wondering how you can beat social phobia or enhance interpersonal skills. The following tips can be handy for becoming more assertive and confident in your workplace.

Show interest

This is a simple rule that many people overlook. You need to show a genuine interest in those you speak with. Don't be self-absorbed and talk only of yourself. This will quickly turn off those around you, and you could become known as a self-centered person.

If you take more interest in others and listen to what they are saying, you can build a good relationship with your colleagues.

Use suitable nonverbal cues

Good conversation does not only depend on what is said; it is also influenced by the way words are said. Nonverbal cues offer a lot of information when you are communicating with someone, and you can convey many things, even without saying a word.

You may offer some great information, but if you deliver it in an unenthusiastic manner, others may also not show any enthusiasm about it. You should not appear to be shy or closed off. Your stance should be confident. You should stand erect, sit with your back straight, and keep your hands on your sides instead of crossing them.

Speak clearly

It is important to speak clearly when conversing with your coworkers. If you feel that your speech is not clear, practice talking at a slower pace. Avoid mumbling as it may seem as if you are not interested in the particular discussion.

Use a tone that is acceptable

Do not speak very loudly and disturb others who are working in the same office. At the same time, you should be careful not to speak so softly that others have to struggle to hear you. If you are unsure about the tone that is permissible, observe your colleagues. Note the tone and pitch that they use to communicate and do the same.

Develop appropriate listening skills

There is a difference between hearing someone and listening actively. For example, you may have experienced that at times when you talk to your coworkers their attention becomes diverted. This may seem quite rude. But sometimes you also do the same thing without realizing it. Therefore, next time when someone talks to you make it a point to listen attentively.

Socialize in a new environment

If you practice socializing in new social settings that are different from the usual ones, it can help you to overcome the anxiety you have about socializing and boost your confidence. Once you become habituated to moving about in different social environments, it will be easier for you to interact with people in your workplace. It may be a good idea to join a dancing class or take up any hobby that interests you. This will give you a chance to mingle with new people.

Be assertive but not aggressive

There is a difference between these two types of behaviors. It is good to assert yourself and put forth your opinions, but you should not be so passionate about it that you go beyond a certain limit when it may seem that you are trying to refute what the other person is saying or trying to prove that they are wrong. If you are on the verge of being offensive, you are entering the aggressive mode.

When the conversation is about to become offensive,

you should just steer it away from that topic and avoid an unwanted heated discussion.

Select the right channels of communication

There are varied ways of communicating with people. Make sure that you choose the right one. For instance, you should never use social media or email for putting forth an argument or conflict. Email does not carry any emotions, and it is difficult to share feelings and empathy through your computer. It is better to talk personally with someone than on the phone. The drawback about written conversation is that even if you use a comma in the wrong place, the meaning can change drastically.

Be flexible and cooperate

It is essential to be flexible and cooperate with others. You should not think that your method of doing things is the only right way. There may be plenty of other methods that other people use that might be equally suitable. You must remember to achieve anything you need the help of other people. You should be willing to share your ideas and also accept the suggestions given by others if they are right.

Do not be defensive and accept criticism

Nobody is perfect, and anyone can make mistakes. You should understand that constructive criticism in the workplace plays an important role in progress, so you should accept it without any bad feelings.

If someone opposes your view or criticizes your work, do

not become defensive. Listen in a composed manner, and do not react immediately. If it is done by someone who has more experience than you, accept it. Although it is not very easy to take criticism, it is a social skill to listen to what is being said in an open manner and be ready to accept it.

Do something that you find challenging

Do the things that you are hesitant about. This will help you to become more sociable. For example, if public speaking is not your strong point, offer to make a presentation or hold a team meeting. It will help you to gain more knowledge as well as experience. You will learn how to deal with such situations.

Show respect to others

You may occupy a high position in your career, but do not forget to be respectful to others. You can give due regard to the feelings of others and show that you care for them as well as honor and admire them. Do not behave as if you possess higher knowledge and experience than the others and they are inferior to you. Being humble and mindful are good social skills that a person should possess.

Practicing good manners or saying "thank you" may make a lot of difference in the interactions with your colleagues. Besides this, you must also respect the personal space of others. Do not be invasive by disturbing them while they are at work or touching them.

Have patience

Patience is a great virtue. It is very useful for the workplace where you have to deal with many people. For example, you should allow the others to finish explaining everything before you jump to conclusions. This can help to avoid misunderstandings as well as confrontations.

Say no to distractions

There are so many things like social media, radio, TV, phones, and tablets that can distract us at work as well as make us separate ourselves from the people around us. To engage yourself sincerely in work and to focus on people who are working with you, it is necessary to avoid these distractions.

Show empathy

Develop the capacity to keep yourself in another person's situation and see things from their point of view. This will enable you to understand and appreciate the things put forth by others.

Be confident

If you have more confidence, you can interact with people better and be more sociable. Other people in the workplace may feel more at ease in approaching you and engaging in conversations with you. Whereas, if you are timid and shy, they may not come to you because they do not want you to feel awkward.

Be a skillful learner

Good entrepreneurs never stop learning. They are always on the lookout for ways things can be done more efficiently and effectively. You should always be ready to learn from others. If you are a good learner, you will be humble and imbibe lessons from the people around you. Your quest for knowledge will enable you to ask questions and get the solutions from experts who love to share their ideas with sincere seekers.

Learn to engage in small talk

It can go a long way in building relationships. Good salesmen have the art of engaging in small talk and making their clients feel special. Small talk portrays your personality effectively and helps you to connect with people beyond the business matters.

CHAPTER - 10

NEXT STEP, HOW TO PROPERLY USE BODY LANGUAGE

The ability to communicate properly is very important for success in any personal or professional relationship. Every time you interact with someone, you convey something verbally and also give a lot of information through the nonverbal cues. Your physical behavior, mannerisms, and expressions that are instinctively done make a great impact on the conversation.

When you are interacting with people, you continuously give and receive wordless signals. These can make others feel at ease, draw them toward you, and build trust. Otherwise, they can confuse, offend and undermine your effort to convey something. You do not stop sending these messages when you become silent. Even during that time you continue to communicate nonverbally.

Sometimes people say something but their body language conveys something else. For example a person may say 'yes' but shake their head as if to say 'no.' When a speaker sends mixed signals like this, the listener may feel that they are being dishonest. Since the nonverbal cues are natural and occur unconsciously, they demonstrate a person's true intentions and feelings. So when the listener has to choose whether to go by your verbal or nonverbal communication, he will pick the latter.

By understanding and using nonverbal communication in a better way, you can convey exactly what you mean, connect well with people and build more rewarding and stronger relationships.

Role of NonVerbal Cues in Communication

- **Compliment:** They compliment or add to what is said. For example, when a boss pats the back of an employee and praises him, the message can have a greater impact.

- **Substitute:** They can act as a substitute for the message that has to be conveyed verbally. For example, a person's facial expression can convey a much more vivid message compared to what is expressed through words.

- **Accent**: They can underline or accentuate the verbal message. For example, if a person pounds the table while speaking, it can make the message appear important.

- **Repeat**: They repeat and strengthen what is said verbally.

- **Contradict:** They can contradict what is being said and indicate that the person is not speaking the truth.

UNDERSTANDING CONCEPTS OF BODY LANGUAGE:

Body language that conveys openness

- In this, a person has a relaxed posture but keeps their back straight. It shows that they are confident and comfortable.

- They keep their legs slightly apart. It demonstrates confidence. They lean in a little while talking to someone to show their interest. They do not lean away because that is a sign of hostility.

- They do not cross their arms. They keep their arms on their sides or keep them together on their lap, which shows that they are open to others.

- Their handshake is assertive and firm. They maintain eye contact. But they do not stare and are not intimidating.

- They speak in a tone that conveys confidence.

Body language that conveys emotions

- If a person's face is flushed, and they clench their fists, it shows they are angry.

- If their face is pale and their mouth is dry so that they drink water or lick their lips, it shows that they are anxious or nervous. Also, their tone of speaking may vary and their muscles may be tense so they might clench their hands or arms. They might show other symptoms of nervousness such as trembling lips, gasping, holding breath, or fidgeting.

153

Body language that shows a person is lying

- A liar may not keep eye contact. Their pupils may appear constricted.

- They might turn their body away.

- A change in complexion, such as redness of face or neck, perspiration, and vocal changes may indicate that a person is lying.

However, some signs like sweating and lack of eye contact can also be indications of fear or nervousness.

Indications of disengagement

- When a person's head is tilted downward or their eyes are gazing elsewhere, it indicates disengagement.

- Fiddling, doodling, and slumping in a chair also show that an individual is disengaged.

Blocking behavior

- If a person crosses their arms or sits behind the monitor of a computer while talking to someone, it exhibits a blocking behavior.

- While giving a speech or presentation, a person may prefer to have some sort of physical barrier between themselves and the audience, such as podiums, chairs, computers or a folder.

Spacing

There are different ideas regarding the amount of physical space that should be given to another person in different cultures. Social distance can be divided into four categories. They are:

- Intimate distance: It is a distance of 1.5 feet from another person. If someone enters the intimate distance of another person, it may be unsettling for them if they have not asked for it. But it may be all right if they are already intimate with each other.

- Personal distance: It is between one to two feet. At this distance, the individuals are quite close; they can shake hands with each other and see their partner's gestures and expressions.

- Social distance: It is between two and four feet. This distance is normally maintained in impersonal situations or during business transactions. In this distance, a person has to speak loudly and eye contact is given importance.

- Public distance: It is between four to six feet. Teachers and those who have to talk to groups usually maintain this distance. In this distance, nonverbal cues are very important but they are often exaggerated. Head movements and hand gestures have a greater significance compared to facial expressions because the latter may not be perceived easily.

Identify your patterns

Think about what you do with your body during the different interactions that you have with various people. You can use a mirror to observe your posture and facial expressions when you are happy, nervous, or angry. In this way, you can identify your patterns of body language.

Assess whether the body language that you use synchronizes with the message you are trying to convey. Your nonverbal cues are effective if they communicate the message that you wish to communicate.

See if there is a disparity, and your posture shows that you lack confidence but your words exhibit confidence.

If your body language matches your words, you will communicate better and also be more charismatic.

USE GESTURES FOR BETTER COMMUNICATION

Hand gestures

Experts say that great speakers make use of hand gestures in the course of presentations and conversations. According to them, these gestures enhance the confidence of the listeners in the particular speaker.

Complex gestures in which both the hands are used above the level of a person's waist are connected to complex thinking.

156 Politicians who are considered to be charismatic and are effective speakers usually use a lot of hand gestures. For

example, Tony Blair, Barack Obama, and Colin Powell are all known to use hand gestures for more effective communication.

However, while using hand gestures you should remember that they should match your intentions and words. Otherwise, they may not convey the right message.

Move around

Great speakers not only move their hands, they also move around in the place. They do not keep themselves distant from people, instead they point to slides and are animated.

If a person keeps their hands in their pockets while speaking, it gives an impression that they are closed off and insecure. It's best to keep your hands out of your pockets, and keep your palms upward. This will show that you can be believed and trusted.

Spot emblems

They refer to gestures that are word equivalents. They may be accepting or passive. You should keep in mind that an emblem can have a different meaning in another culture.

- Tension in a person's body or clenched fists indicate aggression. They show that a person is preparing to fight. Making sudden movements can also show aggression.

- Gentle and slow gestures are considered to be

accepting gestures. Keeping the arms rounded and the palms sideway, which looks like the individual is offering a hug, is an example of such a gesture. It also includes the act of nodding when another person is speaking. It shows that you accept the ideas of the person, and also makes you appear to be an effective listener.

Good posture

When a person maintains a bad posture on important occasions, such as his job interview, they can present a bad impression and perform poorly in the interview. Bad posture is often associated with lack of confidence or engagement and boredom. The interviewer might even think that the person is unmotivated and lazy if they do not sit erect.

To maintain a good posture, you should keep your head up and see to it that your back is straight. You can lean forward when you are sitting and talking to show that you are interested in the conversation.

Mirror the other person

When a person positions themselves in the same manner as the person they're speaking with, it is referred to as mirroring. The idea behind this is that when a person copies their partner's actions, it makes them feel connected.

A person can mirror the other person's body language or tone. But this should be done subtly and not repeatedly or blatantly.

Mirroring is a very effective way of using body language for building a good rapport with another person.

Use gestures to emphasize a point

- Although it is not necessary to make use of a gesture for each word, it is very helpful if you have a number of gestures to convey your messages. You can utilize them to reinforce important concepts that are easily misinterpreted. If the listeners are not able to pick up one gesture, they may surely be acquainted with another one.

- Direct the gestures that are positive toward your listener. This helps you to indicate clearly that you want a positive outcome. You should direct the gestures that are negative away from the listener and yourself. This will help you to clearly show that you do not want any obstacle in conveying your message.

Avoid using gestures that express insecurity or nervousness

- Wandering eyes, picking the fluff on clothing with your hands, and sniffling constantly are some gestures that should be avoided.

- If a person constantly touches their face or is hunched over, they will not look approachable, at ease, or confident. Getting rid of nervous tics takes time. But once they are eliminated, a person's overall communication can improve to a great extent.

DECIPHER FACIAL EXPRESSIONS

Visual dominance

The ratio of visual dominance is determined on the basis of a person looks more at the eyes of the other person and who looks away more. When you are speaking with someone, make an effort to look the person in the eyes to show confidence.

- A person's ratio of visual dominance indicates where he stands in the hierarchy of social dominance compared to his partner with whom he is having a conversation. Those who look away almost all the time have low social dominance.

- Those who mostly look downward show helplessness. It appears as if they are trying to avoid conflict or criticism.

Eye contact can convey different messages

Actually you can learn plenty of things about an individual by observing the way they use their eyes.

- If they avoids eye contact or look downward most of the time, it indicates defensiveness.

- If an individual is making an effort to listen, they will maintain more eye contact.

- If they look away when he is speaking, it suggests that they are not yet in a position to stop talking and listen.

- Looking at another person can also indicate that the

individual is attracted to them. When someone has an interest in another person, their eye contact is strong, and they lean forward toward their partner.

- According to the context, eye contact may be used for showing respect. For instance, during a presentation when there are many people in the room, you can divide the room into three sections. Address your comments to the people on one side, then to those on the opposite side, and finally to those in the middle section. For this you can pick one person in every section and address your comments to them. Those who are seated around these individuals will feel that you are interacting with them directly. This will improve your rating, and you will be an effective speaker.

Emotions are conveyed through facial expressions

You should observe the facial expressions of a person during a conversation. This will help you to know the emotions of the person.

- Facial expressions that offer feedback in the course of a conversation are referred to as regulators. For example, nodding your head or expressions that show boredom or interest. Regulators enable the other individual to evaluate the level of agreement or interest in what is being said.

- You can express empathy toward the other individual through affirmative movements, such as nodding and smiling. If these gestures are used when the other individual is speaking, they provide positive reinforcement to that person and show that you like whatever they are saying.

Improve Your NonVerbal Communication

This sort of communication takes place very rapidly and you have to concentrate fully on what you experience each and every moment. If you plan what should be said next, think about random things or check your phone, you will miss many of the nonverbal cues and fail to comprehend the subtle points that are being communicated.

Besides remaining fully present during the conversation, you need to learn how to handle stress and develop emotional awareness to improve your nonverbal communication.

Manage stress

Stress undermines your capacity to communicate. If you are stressed you may misread the cues that you receive from other people and send confusing nonverbal signals to others. Your behavior patterns may be inappropriate. Emotions are usually contagious. So if you happen to be upset, you make those around you upset and turn a situation from bad to worse.

When you feel stressed, take a few moments to cool down before engaging in the conversation again. After regaining your emotional balance, you will be in a better position to handle things in a more positive way.

Employing your senses to see, smell, hear, touch, and taste is the surest and fastest way to make yourself calm and deal with stress at a particular time. Viewing your child's or pet's photo, smelling your favorite scent, squeezing a stress ball, or listening to music can also help to relax quickly and refocus. Each one can have a different sensory experience that works for them.

Develop emotional awareness

If you want to send the right signals, you must know about your emotions as well as the impact they have on you. You should also have the ability to identify other people's emotions and feelings conveyed by the cues that they send. To do this, you need to have emotional awareness.

If you are emotionally aware it will enable you to:

- Read others accurately, including the nonverbal messages they send and the emotions they experience.

- Gain the trust of people by sending unspoken messages that match your words.

- Show other people that you care for them and understand them by responding in an appropriate manner.

Many people are not able to connect with their strong emotions like fear, sadness, and anger because they have always been told that these feelings should be shut off. However, a person can numb or deny his feelings, but they cannot eliminate them. They continue to exist and affect a person's behavior.

If you become emotionally aware and connect even with the emotions that are unpleasant, you will have more control over the way you think or act. For this, you can practice mindfulness meditation or use some other technique that suits you.

Read the Nonverbal Cues

To gain a proper understanding of what the person is trying to convey, you should not only listen to his words but also observe and assess the nonverbal signs that accompany their speech.

While doing so it is necessary to:

- Observe inconsistencies between the message that is conveyed verbally and nonverbally.

- Look at all the nonverbal cues that you receive in a group from the tone of speaking, eye contact, gestures made by the person, to the position of their body. When they are put together, do they convey the same message as the words that are being said?

- Trust what your instincts tell you.

Evaluate nonverbal signals

- Facial expression: Is the person's face inexpressive and mask-like, or does it show that they are emotionally present and full of interest?

- Eye contact: Observe whether the person's eye contact is just right or overly intense.

- Tone: Does the tone of the individual's voice project confidence, interest, and warmth? Does it appear to be blocked and strained?

- Touch: See if there is some physical contact. Is it suitable for the situation? Is it comforting or discomforting?

- Posture: Is the individual's body immobile and stiff or is it relaxed? Are the shoulders raised and tense, or are they relaxed?

- Intensity: Do they appear to be disinterested and cool, or are they overly excited and melodramatic?

- Sounds: Can you hear any sounds that indicate the person is interested or concerned?

- Timing and pace: Does the conversation flow properly? Do the nonverbal responses appear too slowly or too quickly?

CHAPTER - 11

TIME TO PRACTICE.

HOW TO HAVE A GOOD CONVERSATION

Everyone aspires to have an incredible, dazzling, and memorable conversation. For this, it is important to know how to start a great conversation, continue it in an interesting manner, and end it smoothly.

Ernest Agyemang Yeboah has said, "Sweet conversation is good for the heart and a good pill for forgetting bitter and wasteful thoughts; for a moment, it mutes so many bad thoughts and it keeps the heart calm" (Pills For Healthy Life).

STEPS FOR HAVING A REMARKABLE CONVERSATION

Purpose

You should have a clear goal. Just like you never drive to a new place without knowing the address, you should not engage in a directionless conversation. Indulging in an interaction without a suitable game plan can be compared to driving without being suitably equipped with a map.

If you wish to have a dazzling conversation and get dates

and business connections from your meetings, you should identify your aim before going to events, parties, and meetings.

To be a good conversationalist, you must prepare, practice, and execute like a good athlete with the aim to win. Therefore, you should set your goals, know something about those you are going to meet, and do sufficient research to be well-prepared for the occasion.

While doing this, see if you can answer these questions regarding the event.

Who is the host of the event?

When is the event and what is the agenda?

What type of people will be there?

Why are you going there?

It is all right to have a simple reasons for going there, such as to get new customers or to enjoy time with others. This will enable you to have a purpose while talking with people. Everyone likes people with direction. Purpose is contagious; it gives confidence and enhances influence.

The right approach

Meet people with the right attitude. Approach them as a friend and not as a foe.

Maybe you think that people make their first impression only when they start talking. However, this is a wrong notion. The first impression is made even before that. When the other person sees you for the first time, they notice your confident and open body language.

You should give the right signals of being friendly. For instance, your hands should be visible and shoulders should be relaxed. You can smile and greet people.

Use the technique of bookmarking

You can use this technique to mark or emphasize certain parts of your dialogue that can help in creating deeper connections.

Bookmarks are actually verbal markers that make follow-up easy and give you a topic you can talk about later.

Types of bookmarks:

Future events: While speaking about conferences, if a person you like mentions that they are going to attend a conference in a few weeks and you are also going, you might say that you will be there too and it would be nice to have coffee together after the speeches. You can bookmark it in this way and follow up later.

Interesting incidents: When you are talking with a person and some funny or interesting thing takes place, you can bookmark it and use it later. For example, if you were chatting with someone in the park and you opened a packet of cookies to offer to the other person, and a dog jumped in the middle and sat between both of you, touching your hand with his paw, you might both be surprised by the dog's sudden appearance. Perhaps the dog stayed there and refused to move until he had finished all the cookies, then went away and returned with a ball. The dog put it in front of you and wagged its tail as if to say "Thanks for the treat." You can bookmark it and laugh about it whenever you are about to share some edibles in the future.

Some similarity: Sometimes you may come to know certain things that are similar for both of you. For instance, you may meet someone who has two elder brothers who are two and five years older than them, just like you. You can bookmark it and say that you are lucky to find someone who is in a similar family situation and can understand what it is like to be the youngest in the family and to live with two elder brothers.

Sharing things: When you are talking about articles, books, or videos and someone shows interest in them, you can bookmark it. For example you can say that you will send them the link for it so that they can have a look. This may prompt them to share some of their favorite stuff with you.

Look for something exciting

After you start talking, it is necessary to keep the dialogue interesting, so you should look for some conversation sparks. This is what most of the charismatic people do. They ask questions, introduce topics, and put forth ideas that light up the conversation and kindle excitement.

So try to find the things that the person is excited about and talk about them instead of chit-chatting in a directionless manner and having awkward lulls during the interaction.

Usually, the topic that triggers dopamine makes a person feel excited. So it is a good idea to bring up a topic that enables a person to experience joy.

Some examples of sparking questions are:

- Do you have any plans for a big vacation in the next few months?

- Have you been working on something exciting recently?

- Have you seen any interesting movies recently?

- Are you pursuing some hobbies that you are passionate about?

Nonverbal cues

Raising the eyebrows is an enjoyable trick of nonverbal communication. Almost in all cultures, people raise their eyebrows when they come across something interesting. So if you notice this unspoken cue during a conversation, you should understand that the topic arouses the individual's curiosity, and he may be interested in discussing it.

For example, you may be engaged in a casual conversation about sports. When you mention the name of a certain famous player who studied in your school, the other person may raise their eyebrows. You can guess that he is a fan of that person and talk more about him and hold an interesting conversation.

Tell enchanting stories

Stories make a conversation more captivating. People tend to grasp an idea and remember things more easily with the help of stories or anecdotes. But you should not monopolize the conversation and give a chance to the other person to tell his story as well.

Mutual interaction

Do not hold a lopsided conversation. Even if you tell great stories or exhibit excellent body language, if you do not allow the other person to participate equally, they might avoid talking to you.

There should be reciprocity in a conversation. When a person shares something, they hope that the person they are speaking with will share a similar story. Likewise, when they ask a question, they hope to get a proper answer. So whether you are the speaker or the listener, make sure that there is equal give and take on both sides.

Another mistake to avoid when engaging in a conversation is trying to show that your experience is slightly more than the other person. Do not try to outdo someone. For example, if the other person says that they did not have a good day, you need not say that your day was worse. Or, if they say they have traveled to five countries, you do not need to say you have been to ten countries, even if you have. Give the other person a chance to revel in his own happiness.

End smoothly

Ending the dialogue on a suitable note and making a good last impression also has a lot of significance. You can use the bookmarks you have made earlier for ending your conversation. That means you can touch upon something interesting that you came across during the interaction. Use whatever subject applies to you at the time.

Recollect and analyze

It is quite possible that when you return home after a date or event, you may be very tired and wish to go straight to bed. However, it is advisable to recollect all that took place. You can do this while driving home, talking to your roommate or spouse, or writing a journal.

Try to answer these questions:

- What are the things that went well?

- What did you learn?

- Who is the person you should follow up with?

Recapitulation will help you to learn from your experience and polish your social skills.

CONVERSATION STARTERS

Sometimes, we find ourselves in situations where we aren't quite sure how to start a conversation.

You can use various starters to begin a conversation. You can ask a question or make a comment that can break the ice and start a dialogue with someone.

For example, you can say something about the wine or the venue.

These icebreakers serve as a building block in the formation of relationships, be they short or long term. When we come upon someone new, we can't start out by talking about your daughter's upcoming wedding or how much you enjoyed the latest Netflix flick. These are subjects reserved for those you know well.

To converse with someone you don't know, a comment about the weather is always a good opener that can lead to further conversation. If the person is wearing a sports hat or jacket, and you know something about that particular sport, then you've got a great conversation starter. Sports lovers love to talk about sports.

A sincere compliment is always a great way to strike up a conversation. You must be sincere because pretentiousness will be noticed. You don't want to alienate the person. Give them a chance to expand on the conversation by telling you something about whatever it was you complimented. This will lead to a more engaging conversation.

A psychological trick first described by Ben Franklin is to ask for a favor. For some reason, human nature perhaps, when someone does a favor for another person, it sparks a connection and makes the person more open to conversation. You don't need to ask a stranger anything elaborate. Something as simple as "Can you tell me how to get to room 200?" or "Can I borrow your pen for a moment?" is all you need to say. Most people will be happy to oblige.

Another great opener is to say something about the venue you're at. For example, if you're attending a conference and you see someone you'd like to converse with, you can point something out and make a comment about it. You could mention the seating arrangement or ask where the coffee is located, etc.

If you're in an office setting, you can mention a painting on the wall or construction taking place outside, or anything you see that can spark a discussion. Don't be shy. Most people will respond and be happy to engage in conversation with you.

Asking for someone's opinion is a form of flattery and is a sure way to begin conversing. You can start by saying, "Excuse me, I'm not from here. Could you recommend a good restaurant?" or "I see you have a Starbucks coffee. Do you know how their lattes are?"

All of these things, and more, can open the door to a conversation and a lasting relationship. Even if you never encounter the person again, you likely had an enjoyable exchange and one that made your day a little better.

WAYS TO MAKE YOUR CONVERSATION INTERESTING

Ask something personal in connection with the topic

You've made it through the conversation opener, now you need to keep the discussion moving. The next step is to keep things interesting. You can do this by bringing the conversation around to the other person. People love to talk about themselves, and you want to take the opportunity to do so.

You can segue into a more personal conversation by making the topic about them. For instance, if you're having a generic conversation about the weather, you could ask them if they've ever been to Florida or California, or lived through an earthquake or tornado. You could ask what climate they prefer, if they're sick of living in the cold and snow or if they loathe the heat and humidity.

If you're talking generically about the job market, you can ask what business they're in. There are literally hundreds of topics to discuss that you can gear toward the other person. And when they speak, give them your full attention.

Your goal is to learn more about those you meet, and that's why you'll want to bring the conversation to a more personal level, but not too personal. Asking a stranger if they're married and have children could easily send the person running. You don't want to come off as a creeper. Overly personal questions are out-of-bounds at this stage of the conversation.

Once you have the person talking about themselves, most often they will ask something about you. Don't overdo. This is where you want to contain your excitement that this person has an interest in learning something about you.

You don't want to ramble on about your spouse or kids

or recent vacation, you want to be friendly, concise and answer what was asked of you. Don't use words that some might find offensive or inappropriate. For example, you don't want to tell someone you just met that you just got over a puking spell. This is a surefire way for the person to excuse themselves and head for the hills. And, yes, there are some who will speak that way to a stranger, and you don't want to be counted in that group.

Questions are always good to encourage engagement, and there are a plethora of things you can ask. Stay away from topics that are controversial, such as politics, vaccinations or any topic that can result in a heated debate.

When you attempt a conversation with someone you don't know or someone you've only interacted with briefly, if they aren't interested in talking with you, don't take it personally. Politely excuse yourself and leave.

You have to be aware that not everyone is friendly, or you may have encountered an introvert who isn't comfortable speaking with strangers. It is a normalcy that you're going to run into from time to time. Never force a conversation. If the person doesn't say anything, but their body language sends a message of discomfort, you need to leave the conversation as soon as possible, and politely do so.

Bowing out in a group

Say, you and your coworkers go out for a drink after work. You're all sitting at a table and the conversation turns to the boss. The others are speaking negatively, and you aren't comfortable bashing the boss. You know it could get back to them, and you aren't of the same opinion.

What do you do? You know that soon, one of your coworkers will turn to you and ask you to opine or ask if you agree with something.

This is where the social skill of knowing when to exit comes into play. You can do one of several things to escape. You can pretend you got a text message telling you that you need to leave to pick up one of your kids, or go to your mother's house for something... of course, it's not good to be dishonest but it's worse to have to partake in a conversation that makes you uncomfortable. Added to that, you disagree with what they're saying and that can lead to a debate if you state your feelings. Debates can quickly turn into arguments, especially if those you are with are drinking alcohol. So, it's best to find an excuse to leave.

Just remember your excuse should someone say something to you about it the next day. If a coworker asks if you were on time picking up your son from his baseball practice, you don't want to be caught off-guard and say, "Huh?" That's a sure sign that you fabricated your way out of the group.

CHAPTER - 12

THE DOWNSIDE, HOW TO IMPROVE YOUR LISTENING SKILLS

Appropriate communication is very important in today's highly stressful, high-tech, and high-speed world. Genuine listening is becoming rare because people devote less time to listening to what the other person is saying. Therefore, there is a need to develop good listening skills that can help to build relationships, ensure understanding, resolve conflicts, solve problems, and enhance accuracy.

The less you speak, the more you will hear." - Alexander Solshenitsen

LISTEN ACTIVELY

The outcome of effective listening in the workplace is that less time is wasted and there are fewer errors. The beneficial result of listening actively at home includes the development of self-reliant and resourceful children who have the ability to solve problems on their own. Listening builds careers and friendships. It saves marriages and money.

Here are some tips that can help you in developing good listening skills.

Face the person who is speaking and keep eye contact

Trying to talk to a person who is looking at various things in the room, studying what is given on the screen of a computer, or gazing through the window is like making an effort to hit a moving target. The person's attention is divided between so many things and you may get fifty percent or just five percent of it.

If you were talking to your child, you could ask him to look at you when you are talking. But you cannot order a friend, lover, or colleague to do that.

In the Western culture, eye contact is a basic component of good communication. When you speak, you should look at the other person and they should look at you.

However, this does not mean that a conversation cannot be carried on from different parts of the room. But when the conversation goes on for some time, the people who are speaking will move to the same place to communicate properly.

You should have the courtesy to put away your books, papers, phone, or any other distractions and turn toward the person who is speaking to you. Some people may not be able to maintain eye contact due to shyness, guilt, shame, uncertainty, or cultural taboos. You can excuse them and remain focused. Look at people, and talk even if the others do not do the same with you.

Be attentive and relaxed

After making eye contact, you can relax. There is no need to stare at your partner continually. Look away from time to time when speaking. But you should pay full attention to what is being said.

According to the dictionary to "attend" to another person implies:

- Being present
- Giving attention
- Applying or directing yourself
- Paying attention
- Being ready to do service

Keep all distractions, such as noise and background activity away from your mind. Do not concentrate on the speech mannerisms or accent of the speaker and become distracted. Above all, do not allow your own feelings, biases, and thoughts distract you.

Do not be judgmental

Listen to the other individual without mentally criticizing or judging what they are saying. Do not jump to conclusions. The person who is speaking is expressing their feelings and thoughts through the medium of language. You cannot know their thoughts until you listen to what they are saying.

Do not grab sentences. For example, if you are unable to slow down your mental pace and listen effectively, you may be tempted to rush the speaker by interrupting as they are speaking and finishing their sentences. Such a conversation does not work because both individuals follow their own thoughts and do not know what the other person is actually thinking or trying to say.

Create a picture in your mind

Listen to what the person is saying and make a mental picture based on the information that is being conveyed. If you are focused and your senses are fully alert, your brain can arrange the abstract concepts and give you a clear picture of what is being communicated. If someone speaks for a long time, you can concentrate on the key phrases and words that are used.

During a conversation, when it is your chance to listen to what the other person is saying, do not use that time to plan what you will say next. It is not possible to rehearse what you are going to say and also listen to the other person. You can do only one thing at a time. So you should pay attention only to what the speaker is saying.

Above all, you should focus on what the speaker is saying, even if you are bored. In case your thoughts wander, instantly force your mind to refocus on the speaker's words.

Do not interrupt or impose solutions

It is considered rude if you interrupt when someone is speaking. If a person interrupts it can mean that he is trying to show:

- They are more important.

- They are going to say something that is more accurate, relevant, or interesting.

- They do not care for what the other person thinks.

- They do not have time to listen to the other person's opinion.

- It is not a conversation. It is actually a contest in which he is going to be the winner.

Everyone has a different pace of thinking and speaking. If you can think and talk quickly, it is your responsibility to slow down your pace to match that of the speaker who is slow and more thoughtful, or who has difficulty in expressing himself.

If someone talks to you about their problems, do not start suggesting solutions. Mostly people prefer to find their own solutions. What they actually want from you is to listen. However, if you have a fantastic solution for their problem you can ask them if they would like to know your ideas.

Ask questions when there is a pause

You can ask questions if you do not understand something. But do this when there is a pause instead of interrupting the speaker. You can say that you could not understand what the speaker said about a particular topic.

Do not ask questions and distract the person from the topic

Sometimes it happens that a person is talking about his trip and the exciting things he did there. During the conversation he happens to mention the name of a friend who you have not seen for a long time. Do not start asking too many questions about that friend and his family. This will divert the conversation from the trip that he was describing and make it focus on that mutual friend.

If your question leads the conversation astray, it is your responsibility to bring it back once again to the actual topic. So you can say that it was nice to talk about that friend, but at present you would like to hear more about the person's trip.

Express empathy

Empathy is very important for effective listening. You should feel the way the speaker feels. For example, if the speaker expresses sadness you also feel sad, you feel joyful when he expresses joy, or fearful when he describes his fears. You can convey these feelings through your words or facial expressions.

To experience the feelings of the speaker, you should imagine yourself to be in the speaker's place. This may not be easy, and you may have to concentrate and make a lot of effort to do this.

Chapter 13 go deep into empathy topic.

Give regular feedback

You can show the speaker that you can understand his feelings by saying things that reflect the feelings of the speaker. For example, you can say that the speaker would have been thrilled, or it may have been a great ordeal for the speaker.

If the feelings of the speaker are not clear, you can paraphrase what has been said. You can show through suitable facial expressions that you understand his feelings. In this way, the speaker will know you are paying attention to what is being said and not indulging in some fantasies of your own.

Note the nonverbal cues

We can get to know a lot of things about each other without saying anything. While talking on the phone, we can sense the mood of a person through the tone of their voice. When we talk to a person, we can observe their facial expressions and body language whether they are enthusiastic, bored, or irritated. Therefore, you should not ignore these cues while listening.

THE FIVE-STEP METHOD FOR AN EFFECTIVE LISTENING

The five-step method can help you to acquire the skill of effective listening. For this, you should use a resource that has both audio as well as a written script. First, you should listen to the audio without referring to the text. After that you can use the transcript to check whether you have understood the audio correctly.

You can choose any of the following tools for practice:

- A clip from a TV show or movie along with the subtitles

- An audio book with a printed version

- A podcast with a transcript

- A video from any news site plus a transcript

- A video from YouTube with the available transcription or subtitles

It is ideal to start with one short clip of three to four minutes instead of using a long one. The reasons for doing this are:

- Long clips may be suitable for those who have reached a certain level of advancement, but they can be exhausting for a beginner.

- Repetition occupies an important place in the learning procedure. If the clips are short, it is easier to hear the audio again and again.

- Listening to short clips and learning them well has more value than using longer ones and not gaining in depth knowledge.

Another thing that you should keep in mind while choosing your material is that it should be related to topics that are important to you.

Listen to audio without reading

Listen to audio without reading the text beforehand. Do not refer to it while listening. Focus only on the aural skills. See how far you are able to comprehend without the help of a visual aid.

In the beginning, this exercise may be a little difficult for you, so do not try to understand each and every word that is said, and instead focus on comprehending the gist or the main points of what is spoken.

Note some of the key phrases or words that can help you to understand what is being said.

Repeat

Do not be in a hurry to look at the transcript. Your purpose is to enhance your skills of listening, so continue to focus on listening.

Play the clip once again and listen carefully. There may be some key phrases or words that you may not have noted earlier, make a note of them. Now that you are a little familiar with the context of the piece you may be able to comprehend better.

You should listen to the piece three to four times. You will be able to improve your comprehension bit by bit each time and grasp each word correctly.

Read

After that, you can see the written text. Read it and see whether what you understood through listening is correct. Is the gist that you comprehended correct?

Note whether there are new words and words that sound different when they are spoken. See if you understood them correctly. If you did not follow any of those words, listen to them carefully when you play the audio again.

Use both audio and text

After reading the text and checking the words that you did not comprehend you will have a better understanding of what has been said. The next step is to listen to the piece and refer to the text while listening. You can do this two to three times.

During this stage you will use both aural as well as visual stimuli. You should make the best use of this facility and connect the spoken words to the written words.

Listen to the audio once again

Finally, you should only listen to the audio two to three times without referring to the transcript. By then you may be in a position to grasp everything that is being said without any visual assistance from a text.

CHAPTER - 13

THEY LOVE YOU BECAUSE YOU ARE EMPATHETIC

Empathy refers to the ability of a person to see things through the other person's perspective.

Dale Carnegie said, "If there's one secret of success it lies in the ability to get the other's point of view and see things from that person's angle as well as your own."

A person who is highly empathetic can sense the feelings of the people around him and possesses the capacity to tap into the same feelings within himself. In other words, he is able to truly experience the emotions of the person he is empathizing with.

There is a difference between empathy and sympathy. When a person is sympathetic he pities the other individual and there is some distance between them. But when a person is empathetic, he knows and understands the other person's feelings and also feels the same. So a sympathetic person feels sorry for the other person while an empathetic person feels what the other person is feeling.

Empathy is beneficial for everyone. When a person

expresses empathy, he builds a genuine human connection. The person who receives empathy feels that he is understood, valued, and respected. The empathizer establishes himself as a memorable, trustworthy, and likeable person.

"The most basic of all human needs is the need to understand and be understood." - Ralph Nichols

BEST WAYS TO EXPRESS EMPATHY

Listen

Listening to people is a very effective way of demonstrating empathy. You engage yourself in active listening, which means you listen with a purpose. You paraphrase whatever the person has said and express your emotions. Your emotional reactions form an important component of empathy. They enable the person to regulate his own emotions and responses.

Open up

It is not enough if you just listen to someone, you have to open up emotionally to the person. Only then can you build a deeper connection with them.

Empathy involves sharing vulnerabilities. To practice empathy in the true sense, a person has to share his inner space with someone who reciprocates his feelings.

However, you need not share your life with each and every person you come across. You can choose the person you want to open up to. After identifying the person, you should try to show your feelings regarding a particular topic instead of leaning on opinions in a conversation. Speak in "first person" or use 'I' to start the sentences. For instance, "I am happy we got a chance to spend some time together."

You should never answer a question by saying that you do not know. Make an effort to think of an answer that expresses your feelings. If you absolutely can't think of an answer, you can ask the person you're conversing with to elaborate so that you can provide a better answer. Whatever you do, don't try to "fake it until you make it." The other person will see right through that. You want to do your best to comprehend the question and ask questions if you don't understand.

Show physical affection

It is not possible to do this with everyone. So you should first ask the person if it is all right. The expression of physical affection can enhance the levels of oxytocin. It can make both the individuals feel better.

If you are quite familiar with the person, you can give them a hug, put your arm around their shoulder, or place your hand on their arm. This will show that you are focusing your attention on them and also create a loving connection between both of you.

Oxytocin helps people to interpret the emotions of others in a better way. So a hug may build up both their and your emotional intelligence.

Don't hesitate to ask, "May I give you a hug," or say, "I can take your hand and walk with you."

You never want to place your hands on anyone without knowing that it's okay to do so. If you aren't sure, ask. Don't assume anything. In today's personal space climate, your good intentions can be misinterpreted, and that's the last thing you need.

Notice everything that is going on around you

Focus on your surroundings. Observe the actions, expressions, and feelings of everyone around you. Think about the feelings of the people with whom you interact.

Observe and register the sights, sounds, and smells consciously. Studies have shown that when you practice mindfulness about the people who are near you and your surroundings, there is a greater likelihood of extending empathy toward them and helping someone when he needs it.

Avoid judging others

Judgment, we've already brought that up since is a very important factor when you are practicing mindfulness and empathy.

Generally, people have a tendency to judge others when they meet or interact with them for the first time. But this has to be avoided if you want to be empathetic.

It does not matter whether the person is wrong or right. You have to try to understand his perspective more deeply. This will enable you to develop empathy toward him.

However, this does not mean that you should accept

wrong behavior.

Human nature has us making wrong judgments from time to time. Have you ever met someone and thought right off the bat that you didn't like them? That they were pompous? Have you mistaken shyness for arrogance? We can misjudge others. Often, we can get to know a person better and realize our initial thoughts were completely off-base. This is why you want to avoid passing judgment on someone you just met or don't know well.

We also don't know what the other person might be going through in their personal life. That's why we need to stop judging before we get to know a person.

Offer to help the other person

When you offer help, it is a sign that you are aware of the person's suffering and wish to make their life easier. It is a remarkable expression of empathy. You are ready to spend your precious time on doing something for a person without asking for anything in return.

There are plenty of ways you can help people. You can offer help in simple ways, such as keeping the door open for the next person who is entering a building or buying coffee for someone who is behind you. Also, you can help an elderly person by setting up a computer for them, or you can look after someone's children when they want to go out for some urgent work.

Even if you just offer to help someone, it is an empathetic act. For example, you can open the way for your friend to get support and help from you by saying that if they need anything, they can ask you.

THE RESPONSES TO BE AVOIDED

There are some responses that should be avoided if you wish to be empathetic when a person shares something about his difficult situation with you.

Do not dodge

When someone tells you about their unhappy situation, do not try to shift the conversation to another topic or start checking your phone. Do not try to give an excuse and leave the place in a rush.

The other individual may feel lost and terribly lonely. They might be afraid to open up with anyone in the future.

Look for the silver lining

Some people feel uncomfortable when someone talks about their problems, so they tell that person to look at the brighter side of things. They say that everything happens for a reason.

This sort of response is all right in theory. However, it does not help the person in any way. When a person is in pain, they do not wish to hear all this.

Try to minimize things

When a person talks about their problems, some people try to talk about it in a light manner. They try to make their problems appear smaller so that they may somehow end the conversation. Otherwise, they just keep silent about it and try to convey that the other person is not going through a bad situation. They do not make any attempt to understand or connect with the person's feelings.

Give advice

Usually, when people face medical difficulties, their friends and relatives start offering a number of solutions for their problems. They suggest various therapies and treatments. But they fail to provide the person with what is most needed during such a challenging time. They need someone to listen and be by their side.

Tell stories

Sometimes people feel uncomfortable when a person talks about their struggles, so they start telling a story of a person who faced a similar situation. This may be a harmless gesture, but many times the story that they tell is not very similar and ends badly. So it does not turn out to be helpful or encouraging.

You probably have heard of the pregnant lady who doesn't want to hear another labor story, or how much heartburn they had in the last few months before delivery, or how they know someone who knows the cousin of someone who had gestational diabetes.

Remember, misery doesn't want company, especially when a person is suffering.

Talk about a worse case

As above, there is no use trying to console someone by telling them that there is someone who is going through a worse situation. A person who is suffering cannot gain anything by knowing that their pain is lesser than another. This is such a critical fact to remember. In as much as we think it helps, it doesn't.

Overreact

Do not create a scene and respond in a dramatic manner when someone talks about their woes.

You can sympathize, but don't showcase their troubles. Keep a level head and calm voice at all times.

TIPS TO DEVELOP EMPATHY

Take interest in people

Be interested in knowing about people who aren't in your circle of friends. For example, the people who travel on the public bus with you or those you meet when you are standing in line at a coffee shop.

You should be interested in understanding the other person's world a little. For this, you may have to tell them about yourself and be open.

If someone looks at you, give them a smile. See if there is something in the surroundings that can be used as a pretext to start the conversation. For example, if the person has a book in their hand, you can make a comment about it, or ask the person to help or explain something. You can smile and continue the conversation. If you know the name of the person, you can use it sporadically during the conversation.

However, there are some people who might not like to talk or interact with strangers. For example, they may continue to read a book when you approach them, they may wear headphones, face away from people, or not make eye contact. You should understand their behavior and leave them alone. This is also a part of empathy.

Another thing that you should keep in mind is that you should take due care of yourself while interacting with strangers. Listen to your instincts. If you feel uncomfortable or threatened while talking to a person, stop the interaction and leave.

Work as a volunteer

If you wish to become empathetic toward others you should work as a volunteer. Volunteering can help you to understand people's needs and connect with new people. Dedicating some time to the needy people is also beneficial for a person's mental health.

You can research and find out the organizations where they need volunteers. For example, you can work at any homeless shelter or for an organization like Red Cross.

Overcome your prejudices

Many times it happens that you get stuck with your prejudices. Your notions may not always be right, so you should analyze them. Learn to see each individual in the correct light. Look for something that is similar between you and the other person. Use that similarity to connect with them.

Get rid of your biases, such as those who have mental health problems are dangerous or all those who are poor are lazy or Many of these are based on the wrong information. So acquire proper knowledge about these things.

Imagination

Imagination is very useful for developing empathy toward others. You may not experience everything that the other person goes through; however, you can imagine and get an idea of his feelings. Actively imagining the suffering of another person can enable you to empathize with him.

So when you see an old man begging on the roadside, you should not think that he may spend the money that he is given on alcohol or cigarettes. Instead, you can imagine how they must be feeling because they have to spend their life on the roadside and no one shows any mercy.

It has been found that those who read a lot of fiction are able to understand emotions, intentions, and behaviors in a better way. So it may be helpful to read extensively and develop your imagination.

Experiential empathy

Try to experience someone's life directly by living like them for some time. For example, you can perform all the tasks of your mother for one week. In this way, you can discover the hardships that she has to face in managing the house as well as go out for work. This will enable you to appreciate the amount of work she does and you may decide to help her with the chores.

Give importance to each one

Do not consider yourself to be superior. Each individual has their own importance in the world. Every person has some strengths and some flaws. You should not put them into typical groups and label them.

Meditation

Meditation is not only helpful for dealing with anxiety and stress, it is also useful for developing empathy. You can sit in a quiet place and watch your breath. Visualize that you are worthy of receiving loving kindness. Do not think about your flaws or your strengths.

After getting loving kindness for yourself, practice it for four different kinds of people.

- A person you respect such as a teacher/boss

- A dear one such as a friend or family member

- A neutral individual such as someone at the shop or a person you have seen outside on that day

- A hostile individual such as someone you have disagreed with

To remain on the right track, you can repeat "loving 199

kindness" like a mantra. This will remind you and help you to concentrate on having loving kindness toward all of them, even the hostile individual.

Practicing Empathy in the Workplace

Often, people think that empathy is meant only for their personal lives. According to them, empathy is to be expressed while comforting their daughter who has had a breakup, listening to the woes of a frustrated spouse, pacifying a friend who is mourning, and other such situations.

However, empathy should also be expressed in professional relationships. For example, when you work in a business that is based on referrals and relationships the connections are formed because there is a basic trust between your network and you.

If you show empathy toward people you make them feel that you do not just listen to them but you hear them, and they are understood because they are heard. This makes the people in your network feel connected and safe, so they are able to trust you and your business.

Express vulnerability

Mostly, professional conversations remain within emotionally "safe zones." They stay away from expressing vulnerability.

However, a person should not hesitate to ask someone for help in the workplace. If you ask someone for help you show vulnerability. This vulnerability can often lead to a better connection between you and the other person.

Three steps for showing more vulnerability in professional interactions are:

- After listening carefully to what a person has to say, think about a time when you went through a similar experience. For instance, a project on which you were working might have failed because the team members did not get along with each other.

- Try to recollect the feelings that you experienced at that time. Maybe you were anxious and disappointed.

- Convey those feelings and emotions to them. Then share the things that you learned from the experience.

When you share your own mistakes and insecurities with others, you can connect with them in a much better way.

Do not use assumptions

Assumptions are not suitable when you want to be empathetic. Having assumptions implies that you have preconceived ideas that are formed without experience or true understanding.

As we've already discussed, assumptions are not a good thing. We will look into a couple more reasons why.

Sometimes people try to assume things and take a shortcut to solve problems. But when you take shortcuts, you do not see the complete picture. Consequently, you do not really 'solve' the issue. When you try to solve a problem on the basis of an assumption you may not understand a person's problem correctly. Therefore, the connection that you are trying to make will feel as if it is unnatural and forced.

The person whose problem you are trying to solve may think that you do not understand their problem, and they should not seek your help in future as you do not listen properly. They might withdraw.

You should not try to empathize until you understand the scenario correctly. Spend a little extra time to listen properly and ask questions. Only after that you should try to connect and empathize with others.

CHAPTER - 14

OUTSIDE OF WORK. HOW TO MEET PEOPLE AND MAKE NEW FRIENDS

If you have good friends, your life can be much more enjoyable. You can have fun with them on weekends, go on adventures and trips with them and learn something new from them. You can also share the experiences and stories of your life with them.

In the absence of friends, you may have to live a dull and lonely life. So it is essential to meet people and make friends.

If you want to meet new people you should put yourself in certain social settings where there is more scope for meeting interesting people. You should be in such surroundings where it is easy to socialize. The people you meet will surely bring some joy to you even though all of them may not become your friends ultimately.

OPPORTUNITIES FOR MEETING NEW PEOPLE
Take part in sports

You can join a sports club and take part in various sports and other activities. You may go for hiking or biking with a group of people or become a member of a softball or tennis team.

Look for a group that is involved in a physical activity that you enjoy. Engage the members in a conversation and suggest that you meet for coffee, beer, or wine after the activity or game.

When you go for a hike you can spot the individuals who are sociable and almost the same age as you and start a conversation. It is easy to make friends in beautiful natural surroundings where there are no distractions from day to day life. Moreover, you can share your passion for outdoor sports.

Book clubs

If you are fond of reading, you can join a book club. It will give you a wonderful opportunity to connect with new people who have similar interests like you. If you are interested in joining one you can inquire at the local bookstore or search online. You can join different clubs and see where you can find a group of people who enjoy reading the same books like you and are fond of socializing.

If you do not find the right club that suits your tastes, start a club of your own. Invite people to join it.

Writing groups

If you like to write or have been thinking about it, most communities have writing groups. They are a great way to make new friends and get feedback on your work. If you have a novel inside of you that you haven't started, you will certainly get the encouragement you need from the members of a writing group.

You will enjoy being with like-minded people who are genuine in their wishes for your success. Those in writing groups tend to be very compassionate people, and when you are comfortable being in the group, you can begin to share personal tidbits. Writers are creative people, and not only are they willing to help, they are willing to listen.

Meetup

You can visit MeetUp.com and find various group activities that you might be interested in. Go through the events that are taking place in your area and take part in one or more. For example, you can find networking groups, social groups, and book clubs through Meetup.

Talk to your neighbors

Sometimes we have very nice people who live near us, but we never speak to them and miss the chance of making some good friends. Reach out to them. You may find that they have all the qualities that you are looking for in a friend.

When you see someone who is working in their yard you can offer to help. You can start a conversation about something going on in your neighborhood or community. You can find something in common to talk about, and open the gate from there.

Around the holidays, you can bake cookies or brownies for your neighbors. They will appreciate the kindness.

If you have someone new move in to you neighborhood,

bring them a houseplant, or if weather permits, bring them an outdoor plant. It will make them feel welcome, and they will surely thank you.

Converse with people around you

Wherever you go, whether it is a grocery store, concert or post office, start talking to someone there. You should keep some conversation starters ready with you so that you can break the ice and start talking.

There was once a man at my post office during the holiday rush when line were long, who started doing magic tricks. He entertained everyone in the line and some people took his name and contact information. He utilized his social skills to not only entertain but to make friends. These situations can result in lasting friendships.

You can also be in line at a grocery store and try to small talk the person behind you, who will simply look away from you. These are the people you want to avoid. As stated earlier, don't force yourself on anyone. Turn around and say no more.

Have you ever been in a store and small-talked a cashier who just gives you a blank stare? Those are the most uncomfortable situations, but they do happen and there's nothing you can do except to apologize. You can say, "I'm sorry to have interrupted you. Have a good day."

Use community tables

Look for restaurants that provide the facility for sitting at bar tables or dinner tables. Do not sit in an isolated manner on tables that accommodate just two persons. Sitting at community tables offers a wonderful chance to strike a conversation with strangers seated nearby.

If you stay at a bed and breakfast inn, this is a great way to meet others as the meals are often served with all guests present at the table. You might also share other facilities, such as porch swings and chairs, or boating, etc.

Reach out to people through social media

Visit various social media sites and look for people who live in your area. Reach out to them and ask them out for coffee.

You might discover your old acquaintances or friends who have moved to some place nearby when you go through Facebook. You can reconnect with them.

You can also check the profiles of various people on the social sites and look for those who have something in common with you. Try to contact them and see if they reciprocate properly. You can continue the interaction until you build a good friendship.

You want to be careful, and always meet in a public place. You don't need to put yourself in danger. And never give too much personal information if the person is unknown to you. Be sure if you're going to meet with a stranger that you met online that you let someone know where you will be and the time you will be there. Better yet, have a friend nearby. For instance, if you meet at a coffee shop, have a friend sitting in the shop when you arrive. You need to pretend you don't know them.

And as many of us have done in the past when we are with someone we might not want to be with, have a friend call or text with a reason to leave. That works every time!

Host a party

You can host a casual party and invite people who live in your neighborhood, work in the same place as you, or acquaintances. Tell them that they can bring their friends along with them. This will increase the scope of meeting new people or potential friends.

You need not have an elaborate party. Even some soup and pizzas are sufficient. The aim is to make people come together and to expand your social circle.

Go for a walk with your dog

If you have a dog, when you go walking, surely, there will be people who will stop to admire it and ask you questions about breed, gender, etc. It will give people an excuse to start a conversation with you. Moreover, there may be other people who are taking their pets out for a walk. Your pet may attract the attention of those pets who may drag their masters to you. This may give you a chance to meet new people.

If you are lucky to have a park for dogs in the area, you can take a frisbee or ball with you when you take your pet there for an outing. This may give you a chance to mingle and make friends with other dog lovers over there.

Business associations

Connect with associations or groups that are associated with your career. You can research and find out the business events that are going on in your area. Attend them and connect with the other participants professionally as well as personally.

Most professions have organizations. Lawyers have bar associations, the media has press clubs, teachers have associations as do business owners. Don't be shy. Join and volunteer.

Go to the gym

A gym is a very suitable place for meeting new people. When you attend a gym class, you get a chance to meet many new people who are interested in doing physical exercise, losing weight, or are health conscious just like you.

If there is a juice bar or cafe at the gym, you can hang out with the others after completing your workout.

The same goes for exercise classes. Whether it's Zumba or Crossfit or Parkour or even a snowshoeing class or canoeing class, you're bound to meet many new people.

Ask someone to introduce you to friends

If some of your friends have a wide social circle you can ask them for introductions. For example, if you move to another place you may not know many people. At such times, you can ask your close friend who already knows a lot of people there to make an introduction. They can send an email to their friends and introduce you. Then you can follow up and meet them for coffee or dinner.

Join a speaking club

Mostly, public speaking is not everyone's cup of tea. But when you join a speaking club you are with a group of people who have the same learning curve and similar fears. This gives them a common ground to interact more freely with each other.

Speaking clubs help a person to become more confident about making presentations and also give him an opportunity to meet various interesting people.

Toastmasters is one such organization for public speaking, and you will meet many people will a common interest.

Attend cultural events

You can become a member of the local theater, symphony, or ballet group. Attend the fundraising events and the performances. Start conversations with other people who come to attend the function. They come because they also appreciate art like you. So you may find something common to strike a friendship.

If you are fond of visual art you can visit the local galleries or exhibitions and discuss art with the organizers or guests.

Brew tours

If you live in some place where there a number of breweries you can join a brew tour. Many wineries and restaurants offer wine tasting facility. By participating in a beer or wine tour you can meet connoisseurs and also have fun. Beer and wine always pair well with socializing.

Attend seminars

Take a look at the local community calendar and find the events that are going to take place in the area. Attend the seminars and other functions. While doing so try to find a seat next to a person who may also be on the lookout for a friend like you.

Go to a music club

If you are a lover of music and like jazz or any other genre that is suitable for having a conversation in a small place you can join a low key music club. You can have a great conversation with new people and also enjoy great music.

Dance classes

Ballroom dancing gives an opportunity to get close to new friends and have personal contact with romantic partners. However, it is not necessary to stick to ballroom dance alone. You can join a class for learning Salsa dancing or Zumba. It is great for exercising as well as for meeting people who love to have fun.

Visit a museum

Usually there are several museums in cities that cater to the interests of different people. For those who are fond of art, science or natural history, a museum can be a very suitable place for meeting new people. You can talk to other people who come to visit the museum and chat about the things that you have seen.

Art classes

When you join any class, you automatically come into contact with many people who have similar interests. You can enroll in an art class where you have to do things together instead of listening to a lecture. This will give you a chance to converse with the other students. You should introduce yourself and initiate a conversation with them.

Whether it's watercolor or pottery classes, you can interact with the participants. It's a great way to meet others and to get feedback on your work and give others feedback.

Join a nonprofit organization

Those who like to support a cause that is particularly meaningful for them can become a member of a charitable association. As a decision-maker or leader in such an organization they can meet a wide variety of people who extend their support for the same cause.

Coffee house

If you work from home you may have to stay in your house most of the time. That means you may not be able to meet any new people or make friends. So you should take your computer to a local coffee house and do your work there. You can continue your work and also look up once in a while to survey the people who come and go. It is also possible to talk to the person who is sitting on the table beside you. This person could become a good friend.

Go to a bar

You may find it intimidating to dine alone at a restaurant. You can go to the bar and have a conversation with the bartender as well as the other people who are there. Remember, don't sit and look at your phone or read a book. Instead, be friendly and approachable.

Make the best use of invitations

Do not turn down any invitations that you may get for social events. They offer a great opportunity to meet people. Even if the event is about something in which you are not at all interested do not miss it. If you do not like it you can leave whenever you like.

Visit a farmers' market

If you are fond of eating healthy food and enjoy cooking, farmers' markets can be fun for you. There you will find lots of people who have similar food values like you.

It will give you a chance to speak to the farmers, ask them

questions, and also have a conversation with the other shoppers. There is a festive and sociable atmosphere at such events. You should take advantage of them and meet new people.

Don't skip your class reunion

Class reunions are a great way to rekindle old friendships and make new ones. If you went to a large school, chances are you never got to know all of your classmates. It's a perfect way to reacquaint yourself with classmates.

Chances are you won't run out of things to talk about, as reminiscing about school days is a subject most people enjoy, especially at reunions. Talking about the past and learning what your classmates are doing and hearing about their families and jobs is fun, and it can reestablish connections that were lost with time.

The more years that pass, the more classmates will generally show up for reunions. Make it a point to attend them all. If you were shy in school, and are not longer that same person, you can show how you've evolved over the years.

SMART WAYS OF MAKING FRIENDS

There are six important steps to meet people and make friends quickly. They are:

- Identify your favorite subject, hobby, or sport.

- Find the meetup groups or forums associated with that subject.

- Pick out the interest groups which meet regularly for

discussing the subject.

- Participate in their meetings.

- Speak about things such as when was it that you started liking the subject or hobby, and how frequently you engage yourself in it.

- Jump to another conversation topic that is not connected with the key subject.

Basic requirement for starting a friendship quickly

Sometimes people follow all the steps mentioned above, but even then they are not able to make new friends. The main reason for this is, it is not enough to have just one thing in common with the other person, two commonalities are needed for creating a friendship.

Whenever you take part in a social gathering and meet new people try to find the other common things between you besides the key subject for which the meeting is taking place.

The formula is as follows:

Potential friendship = 1st commonality + 2nd commonality

TIPS FOR MAKING FRIENDS

If you wish to socialize you have to take the initiative. You cannot wait for someone to approach you. It is not that such things never happen. They do occur but they are rare. You have to make an effort to find friends:

Do not waste the weekend on frivolous tasks and hope

that someone will text you. Instead of this, you should contact different people and find out their plans. See if it is feasible to join them. Otherwise, you can make a plan and ask others to join you. Do not hesitate to ask for company and think that it may look as if you are needy or desperate. In fact, it shows that you are a social person.

If others seem to be indifferent toward you, don't feel hurt. Many times people are too preoccupied and forget to include you in their social activities. It does not imply that they would not like to have you around them. Maybe you need to show more interest in their social activities to gain their attention.

Similarly, there may be some people who are slow in replying to emails or calling back. If you do not get an answer or if you get a delayed answer do not assume that they are trying to ignore or reject you. There is that word again–assume. It can't be stressed enough how bad assumptions are.

Do not be under the impression that it is very difficult to make friends. It is not as complex as you imagine it to be. Get rid of the inhibitions that you have about friendship.

You just need to meet someone you can get along and spend quality time with. It is not necessary to know each other for a very long time before becoming friends. Even if your relationship is not very deep or intimate, you can have a nice time and enjoy each other's company.

216 Do not be choosy if you are building your social circle

from scratch. If you feel lonely, your first goal is to find someone who can give you company. So if you come across someone who is nice but not hundred percent ideal for being a friend, you can try to make friends with them. However, you should stay away from people who are toxic.

Socializing with people who are not as perfect as you want your friends to be is much better than staying alone and moping. Besides this, until you mix with different people you may not know much about people and their ways of interacting. Moreover, if you have a few friends it becomes easier to make more friends and expanding your social circle.

People who are lonely usually have a negative view of others. Those who are not the outgoing type are more choosy about the people they spend time with. So if you happen to be that kind of a person, try to overcome this attitude. Above all, you should not have a skewed image of yourself. Be realistic and understand your needs and circumstances correctly.

Another reason why a person may not like to hang around with someone is that they might have a very poor image of themselves and the other person seems to mirror their shortcomings. This is justified if they have some pesky traits and want to avoid those who have similar traits. However, there is a possibility of turning away some good individuals who happen to possess a few characteristics that tweak that person's insecurities slightly.

Don't get discouraged easily, and be persistent. When you join a club or your friend introduces you to his friends you may look forward to mixing with some wonderful people. But after you go there or mix with them, you have a disappointing experience. You start feeling that you lack the skills necessary for making friends. You may think that they are ignoring you or making fun of you.

But you should not give up so easily. Try mixing with these groups again. Often, the initial meeting may not be sufficient to connect with others properly.

If an individual does not accept your invitation as he is busy, do not get disheartened. Try again some other time. Do not jump to conclusions and assume that they don't like you or that no one likes you.

By giving an invitation, you have conveyed to the other person that you are fond of them. They might not be able to meet you this time, but they will start seeing you as a person they can have an enjoyable time with on some other occasion.

Be realistic while meeting a potential friend. Think about the place you occupy in their life and how much time it will take to become good friends. Be patient and wait for the right opportunity. If you are in a situation that is suitable for finding and making friends such as a college, team or club, it may not take much time to make friends.

In other situations, you may have to spend some time looking for like-minded people. After that, you may have to meet for some months to know each other properly. It may take a year to become really good friends.

If you have enough patience you can progress from the stage when you have no plans at all to the stage of having plans for every weekend with one person, to the next stage of having plans for two days every week with a number of people.

TOP FRIEND MAKING HACKS FOR SHY PEOPLE

Sometimes people who are shy wonder how they can make friends. It's a lot harder for those who are more reserved and feel awkward around others. It's not impossible to make friends, but it is more difficult.

For those who are shy, it's important that they socialize within their limits. This means not stepping out more than they are ready to do. It can take practice and self-confidence to meet others and feel relaxed.

For those who are timid, it can help to be in a group setting. That way, you won't have the awkwardness of a one-on-one conversation if things start going south.

When in a group, there's always someone to save you. Group settings can help you to become comfortable being around others, it can help you to overcome your shyness, and it can be a confidence-builder.

When you're in a social setting with a group of people, look approachable. That means to stand or sit in a position so that your body language tells others you're willing to have a conversation. You don't want to be a wallflower or sit with your hand covering a part of your face. You'll want to show some confidence, even if you aren't feeling it.

You should stand or sit so that you are visible to others. Someone might approach you who will do the following:

- Guide the conversation in such a way that you can open up.

- Attempt to make you feel comfortable.

- Invite you to meet their friends.

- Make you feel a part of whatever it is that's going on.

Approaching a shy person

When we see a shy person, we might want to approach them, especially if they look uncomfortable in a social setting.

Before you approach someone, you might want to ask around, in a stealth way, who the person is. They are there for a reason, and someone invited them, so you can learn something about that person before approaching them.

Say, for example, a friend tells you that they work with the shy person and they are an amazing artist. You now have a segue for your approach, especially if you know something about art.

Getting to know something about the person you want to approach makes for a more comfortable encounter.

You'll be able to read the person to know if they are

interested in conversing or if you need to bow out gracefully.

This is something that can't be stressed enough. There are people who just don't want to be approached. They are content to be in their own world. They are enjoying themselves even if they don't appear to be.

There's nothing wrong with being a loner. It can't hold you back from certain things in life, but if that's your level of comfort, then don't feel guilty about it. As long as a person doesn't feel isolated and sink into a depression, keeping oneself company is not atypical.

We hear all the time about men who have "man caves," where they go for their alone time, away from family and life. We have all heard about women who lock themselves in their sewing rooms and get lost for hours in their projects. Everyone needs alone time, and there's nothing wrong with it.

When alone time turns to constants isolation, that's when it's best to seek professional help.

Whether you're shy or you want to approach someone who appears to be shy, remember our tips.

Friendships can be made and had with shy people. And you might be surprised how they will open up once they get to know you. Again, it can't be stressed enough– don't mistake shyness for arrogance. Timid people can send the wrong vibes, and you could miss out on an opportunity to make a great friend.

CONCLUSION

Relationships can be a lot of work. They can be demanding, nerve-wrecking, and hurtful. They require love, care, understanding, and appreciation. The aim of this book is to help you understand yours and take whatever necessary measures it requires to keep it enriched and nourished. Keep in mind that it is only you and your partner who have to do all the work as a team. There will be critics around you, people suggesting you how you should work out your finances, raise the kids, do stuff together to stay bonded, and everything. But don't assume those suggestions as a standard that you have to maintain or live up you. What you and your partner have is unique. Don't try to perfect it with someone else's idea of perfection. Do what is best for your family and more importantly, you two.

Let this guide help you to find your own path to succeed in your relationship. Let this help you work out the differences you two have. Let it show you how to handle criticism, conflicts, and arguments. Let it tell you how to appreciate, communicate and love more deeply. Let it 223 make way for you to forgive when wronged and rebuild with a clean slate.

And most importantly, let it teach you how to communicate with your spouse on a secondary level without any fear of rejection, judgment, or failure. The only failure is not expressing emotions and feelings openly so don't make that mistake.